Favorite
FAMILY RECIPES

MOST REQUESTED
COPYCAT
DISHES

Favorite
FAMILY RECIPES

MOST REQUESTED
COPYCAT
DISHES

101 Homemade Versions of Your Favorite Restaurant Recipes

SHADOW
MOUNTAIN
PUBLISHING

Photo by Makayla Madden Photography

To our mom, Linda K. Edwards, whose commitment to gathering her family for dinner every night has blessed generations. Her creativity in the kitchen has been a continuous source of inspiration. We love you, Mom.

Food photography by Heidi Rasmussen, Kelsey Crist, and Erica Walker. Photo on page 10 by Echo Walker.

Visit us at shadowmountain.com

Library of Congress Cataloging-in-Publication Data

Names: Favorite Family Recipes (Bloggers), author.
Title: Most requested copycat dishes : 101 homemade versions of your favorite restaurant recipes / Favorite Family Recipes.
Description: Salt Lake City : Shadow Mountain, [2024] | Includes index. | Summary: "Unravel the culinary secrets behind your most-loved restaurant meals. From fast-food classics to gourmet restaurant delights, *Most Requested Copycat Dishes* brings the restaurant experience directly to your home kitchen."—Provided by publisher.
Identifiers: LCCN 2024011027 (print) | LCCN 2024011028 (ebook) | ISBN 9781639933198 (trade paperback) | ISBN 9781649332936 (ebook)
Subjects: LCSH: Cooking, American. | Chain restaurants—United States. | BISAC: COOKING / Comfort Food | COOKING / Methods / Quick & Easy | LCGFT: Copycat cookbooks.
Classification: LCC TX715 .M917 2024 (print) | LCC TX715 (ebook) | DDC 641.5973—dc23/eng/20240415
LC record available at https://lccn.loc.gov/2024011027
LC ebook record available at https://lccn.loc.gov/2024011028

Printed in China
RR Donnelley, Dongguan, China

10 9 8 7 6 5 4 3 2 1

CONTENTS

INTRODUCTION

TOP TEN TIPS FOR CREATING
YOUR OWN COPYCAT RECIPES

by Erica Walker

Re-creating versions of your restaurant favorites can be easy and fun. With these simple tools and instructions, you'll soon be busy making the foods you love.

1. BE OBSERVANT

There's a restaurant in Boise, Idaho, that serves up the best tableside guacamole I have ever tasted. After my first time eating there, I knew I had to find out how to make it on my own. So the next time I went to the restaurant, I paid close attention to how they made it. I took note of each and every ingredient and the order in which they were added. One thing that stood out to me was the fact that the restaurant used green tabasco sauce. I counted exactly how many shakes were used. I then estimated the amount of ingredients—a half cup of diced tomatoes, exactly three avocados, a generous pinch of salt. I tried it at home the following night, and it worked! It tasted exactly like that delicious guacamole from the restaurant.

When you go to a fast, casual restaurant like Chipotle or Cafe Rio, where you order at the counter, pay attention to what's going on in the kitchen. How are they grilling their chicken? Can you tell what seasonings they're putting in the marinade? Most restaurants use simple, fresh ingredients that are relatively easy to replicate at home. One of my favorite Cafe Rio dishes is their delectable tortilla soup. I noticed all they did was add a couple ladles of broth over a scoop of beans and guacamole, both of which I already had copycat recipes for. Once I figured out the broth recipe, which wasn't hard to do, I had a pretty decent version of that warm, comforting soup without ever leaving my cozy kitchen.

Another huge fan favorite dish at Cafe Rio is their sweet pork. A couple of years ago, I was standing in line, anticipating my pork salad, when I saw one of the workers come out to the soda machine with a big white bucket. He proceeded to fill it to the brim with Coca-Cola. Either he had a big thirst to quench, or he was going to use it as an ingredient. Sure enough, he pulled out a huge plastic bin of tender pork, poured the soda over it, and snapped the lid shut. I always knew the secret to sweet pork was soda; some copycat recipes called for Dr Pepper, Diet Coke, or even root beer. Nope. I saw it with my own eyes—straight up, regular Coca-Cola. So that's what we use for our copycat recipe, and it tastes just like the original.

Every time you go out to eat, keep your eyes peeled for clues. They're just waiting to be discovered and put to use in your own kitchen.

2. ASK QUESTIONS (GRILL YOUR SERVER)

While traveling in southern Utah, I requested a to-go order at my favorite sandwich place. I adore the sauce they put on their sandwiches! For ages, I've tried to figure out their sauce recipe; there was a certain flavor I couldn't quite put my taste buds on. So when the employee asked if I wanted their special sauce on my order, I asked, "Maybe. What's in it?" Without hesitation, the employee gave me a rundown of the ingredients—including *saffron*! I never would have guessed it, but since I knew I could figure out the rest of the ingredients, I also knew my home-made sandwiches would never be the same.

A couple years ago, I spent a glorious date night at the Melting Pot with my husband. The fondue was delicious, and I kept trying to figure out what was in it. I had seen the actual Melting Pot cookbook and knew this recipe wasn't in it, so I asked our waiter for the recipe. He said it was one of his favorites, too. He pulled out a napkin and wrote it down for me from memory!

Many people deal with food allergies, so what used to be hard-to-find information is now freely shared in restaurants to keep diners safe and healthy. Unless it's a super-secret ingredient or recipe, restaurant workers will usually tell you what's in a sauce or dressing. When I worked in a restaurant years ago, I was asked many times what was in a sauce or soup, dip or dressing. I told the customer every single ingredient to the best of my knowledge. And if I didn't know, I asked a manager or the chef. I didn't want a customer angry that I didn't disclose an ingredient that might cause an allergic reaction.

So, ask away, and armed with your newfound knowledge, practice at home with the ingredient proportions until you get it right.

3. CHECK THE RESTAURANT WEBSITE FOR A MENU OR CONTACT THE RESTAURANT

Did you know that the ingredient list to your favorite meal could be just a mouse click away? Many restaurants publish their menu online, including ingredient and nutrition information. When I set out to make a copycat dish from Rumbi Island Grill, I went online and, lo and behold, there were all the ingredients listed. If the restaurant doesn't have the dish's exact ingredients online, try emailing the restaurant. Often they will give you the recipe, no questions asked.

4. COME UP WITH A STARTING POINT

If you want to re-create the mushroom sauce from that one place you ate at that one time, you don't have to create it from scratch. Chances are the mushroom sauce is similar to other mushroom sauce recipes out there. Start with a comparable recipe as a template and use that to determine the similarities and differences. It can make unlocking the recipe so much easier.

When trying to figure out a dressing, sauce, or soup, start with the base first and then work from there. For example, is the salad dressing creamy or vinegar-based? If it's got a creamy texture, chances are the recipe calls for mayonnaise, sour cream, or Greek yogurt. If a raspberry vinaigrette caught your attention at lunch the other day, start with vinegar and oil.

If you're trying to replicate soup from your favorite lunch counter, use the same method. Creamy soups generally begin with a roux and/or half-and-half or heavy cream. Brothy soups will feature either beef, chicken, or vegetable broths. Taste all three kinds and get to know the difference so you can more easily identify which is used in your favorite restaurant soup.

5. KNOW YOUR HERBS AND SPICES

It sometimes takes just the tiniest addition of spice to take a dish from ordinary to extraordinary. Food is always better when it's seasoned the right way, so become familiar with as many herbs and spices as you can. How do they taste? How do they smell? How do they look? How are certain herbs best prepared?

Herbs like parsley, oregano, or cilantro—whether fresh or dried—are best used with oil or water so they can infuse the liquid while cooking. Spices like nutmeg, cinnamon, or ginger are more potent and are almost always used in their dried form. Figure out what spices pair well with different kinds of meats, fruits, veggies, or cheeses. Then see how various blends of spices fit together. Experimentation is key.

Keep your spices handy when creating your recipe. You'll need to know how spices smell and taste individually if you're going to pick them out of a recipe once everything is blended together. Do you know what a soup tastes like with an added bay leaf as opposed to one without it?

Use your eyes in addition to your nose. Look closely at the food you're trying to duplicate for clues. Do you see any green specks? Those could be parsley, cilantro, basil, or oregano. Is there a red tint to it? The dish may have chili powder or paprika. How about a yellow tint? Try turmeric or curry. I find that soups are the easiest to figure out visually. A lot of the time, herbs are coarsely chopped, making them easier to identify.

6. KNOW YOUR GLOBAL CUISINES

Where in the world is your dish from? Becoming familiar with cooking traditions and practices from different regions of the world can help tremendously when you are picking apart a recipe. A cuisine is primarily influenced by the ingredients available in that area. Learn what herbs and spices are generally used when preparing a dish from a specific region. For example, if your favorite Korean restaurant has a dish you can't get out of your mind, learn about the spices, herbs, and foods that are popular in that area of the world. It's unlikely that you'll find curry in an Italian dish or oregano in a Chinese meal. If this feels like a lot of information,

HERBS AND SPICES BY REGION

MEXICAN
Garlic
Oregano
Cayenne
Cilantro
Coriander
Cumin
Allspice
Chili powder
Crushed red pepper
Dried chiles
 Guajillo, Chipotle,
 Puya, Chiles de Arbol,
 Pequin, Ancho, Pasilla

CHINESE
Ginger
Garlic
Star Anise
Five-Spice powder
Sichuan peppercorn
Fennel
Cloves
Cinnamon

INDIAN
Turmeric
Cumin
Curry powder
Cardamom
Cilantro
Coriander
 (dried cilantro seed)
Garam Masala
Ginger
Garlic
Fenugreek
Cinnamon
Fennel
Star Anise
Nutmeg
Cloves
Mustard seed
Indian red chili

FRENCH
Herbes de Provence
Rosemary
Oregano
Bay leaves
Marjoram
Nutmeg
Tarragon
Saffron
Parsley
Chives
Chervil
Basil
Pepper (white & black)

ITALIAN
Garlic
Basil
Oregano
Parsley
Marjoram
Parsley
Chili pepper
Rosemary
Thyme
Sage
Bay leaves

GREEK/ MEDITERRANEAN
Oregano
Mint
Garlic
Onion
Dill
Bay leaves
Basil
Thyme
Fennel seed
Parsley

THAI
Lemongrass
Ginger
Chili
Garlic
Coriander
 (dried cilantro seed)
Cinnamon
Pepper
Cumin
Kaffir lime leaves
Star Anise
Clove
Mace

don't worry! There are a lot of great websites online that list what spices are typically used in dishes all over the world.

7. TASTE AS YOU GO AND TAKE NOTES

This one is really important. Don't rely on your memory alone when duplicating a recipe. I can't tell you how many times I worked out a recipe but forgot to write down *exactly* what I did! Every time you add something, write it down. Be as accurate as possible so you can duplicate the process again.

Always start with small quantities of seasonings and add more as you go. It may be cliche, but it's always easier to add more of an ingredient than to try to take it away.

Remember that some recipes take more time and effort to duplicate and perfect. There are many recipes where you can't just keep adding ingredients and testing side by side until you get it right. For example, you won't be able to determine the success of a cake until it's out of the oven, and by then, it's too late to add an ingredient or two. That's why writing down every ingredient, amount, and method is so important. That way, the next time you need to change up the recipe, you can go back to your notes (be it version one or one hundred) and see exactly what you did. I like to write my new adjustments or suggestions in a different color so when I rework a recipe, I know if those particular adjustments got me closer to my goal or further away.

8. DO A SIDE-BY-SIDE COMPARISON

The next time you are out to eat, order some of your favorites to go and then take them home to compare alongside your creations. Your family will thank you for the leftovers, trust me. If the restaurant sells their sauces or dressings separately, snatch up a bottle and get to experimenting in your kitchen. When I was trying to figure out the sauce for my favorite rice bowls from Rumbi Island Grill, I bought a container of their sauce to use as my base. I kept comparing it, side by side, and added ingredients as necessary. You might be surprised by how quickly you can pick out differences between the two. You may notice the original is sweeter than the one you are creating, or saltier, or spicier, and you can adjust yours accordingly until you get it right.

9. GET FEEDBACK

There will come a point where you are sick of comparing your own recipe to the original. You may sense that you are getting close but that you're not 100% there, but you can't possibly eat that chicken diablo recipe anymore! That's when you need to get a second or third (or fourth or fifth) opinion. Tell your "taste testers" to be brutally honest. Often, they will be able to pick out an ingredient or two that you overlooked. They may tell you your version is not even close and you should start over again. (That has happened to me many times!) But practice makes perfect, and I suspect your taste testers wouldn't mind sampling a few more brownies. Asking for feedback is a wonderful way to get the family into the kitchen and involved in this process. And who knows—you could find new family favorites as you experiment together.

10. LOOK ONLINE

I saved this tip for last because I really want to encourage you to hold off looking online for answers if you can. Places like Reddit can be a great resource, but they can also be misleading. Sometimes, I have found recipes and methods online for recipes from actual restaurant employees. Other times, I have found recipes that were way off or even information that was misleading.

A few years ago, I was working on duplicating the Panda Express chow mein recipe. I got as far as I could and then consulted an online source that claimed to be the *actual* recipe. But when I read through the ingredients, I noticed the recipe called for carrots, bean sprouts, and green onions—none of which are truly in the actual recipe (as I saw when I consulted the Panda Express menu online).

If you are really struggling with a recipe, it doesn't hurt to post a question in an online forum to see if you can find someone who knows the actual recipe you are looking for, but I wouldn't put all my stock in the answers you get. Trust your instincts, and don't let other copycat recipes bias your own good judgment. Be confident in your taste buds and get as close as you can before consulting the internet or other copycat recipes for answers.

IN CONCLUSION

Achieving the perfect copycat recipe might take time. Don't rush the process. Enjoy the journey of experimentation and improvement. Don't expect 100% accuracy all the time. Restaurants wouldn't stay in business very long if their recipes were easy to replicate. You may try several times and still not be able to figure out that "secret" ingredient. Or you may not be willing to make a dish with the high amounts of salt, butter, sugar, or fat that makes those restaurant meals taste so good.

Keep trying! And remember, developing recipes is a practice in patience. I am still working on recipes that I started months ago. Enjoy the failed recipes as best you can and try again. Don't get frustrated. One day you will hit the nail on the head and call all your friends to announce the new recipe you created (well, duplicated). Happy cooking!

DRINKS AND SHAKES

CARAMEL APPLE SPICE CIDER

Inspired by **Starbucks**

TOTAL TIME: 5 MIN · SERVES 1

This Starbucks caramel apple spice cider copycat is my fall drink of choice! This delicious warm apple cider drink is *the* actual recipe used at Starbucks.

Caramel Apple Spice Cider

1 cup apple juice

1 tablespoon Starbucks Cinnamon Dolce Syrup or Torani Brown Sugar Cinnamon Syrup

Toppings

whipped cream

caramel topping

ground cinnamon

cinnamon stick

1. Combine apple juice and syrup in a small saucepan. Heat on the stovetop to desired temperature. It does not need to boil. You can also heat it in the microwave.

2. Top with whipped cream and caramel topping. Add a few dashes of cinnamon and a cinnamon stick for garnish.

NOTES

• You can find Torani or DaVinci cinnamon syrup for a fraction of the price of the Starbucks brand. Just use the same amounts as mentioned in the recipe. As an alternative, you can make your own syrup by combining ½ cup water, ½ cup brown sugar, and 1 teaspoon cinnamon in a small pot and simmering over medium heat for 5 minutes, until it reduces.

• A lot of our readers like making their own whipped cream. You can do this by using a hand mixer or stand mixer. Beat 2 cups heavy cream with a few tablespoons of granulated sugar until it reaches desired consistency.

PUMPKIN SPICE STEAMER

Inspired by **Starbucks**

PREP TIME: 5 MIN · COOK TIME: 5 MIN · TOTAL TIME: 10 MIN · SERVES 4

These pumpkin steamers will warm you on a cold autumn day. So instead of swinging through a drive-thru, whip up a batch of this rich and creamy comfort drink to satisfy that beverage craving.

Pumpkin Spice Steamer

3 cups milk (2% or whole)

1 cup heavy whipping cream

½ cup pumpkin puree

½ cup brown sugar

2 tablespoons sweetened condensed milk

2 teaspoons pumpkin pie spice

2 teaspoons vanilla extract

Topping

whipped cream

ground cinnamon

1. Blend all steamer ingredients in a blender until smooth and frothy.
2. Pour into a large pot. Heat on medium-high, stirring constantly, until warmed through, about 5 minutes. Make sure to stir so the milk doesn't scald or boil.
3. Pour into mugs, top with whipped cream, and sprinkle with cinnamon.

NOTES

• When we serve this drink at a party, we like to leave it in a slow cooker on the warm setting. Throughout the party, make sure to stir it so the spices don't settle at the bottom.

• When you are making this recipe, you can play with the balance of milk and heavy cream or even try half-and-half, depending on how creamy you like your hot drinks. If you'd rather make it dairy-free, you can try oat milk or almond milk instead.

• It is best to simmer this drink in a heavy-bottom saucepan on low heat.

COPYCAT SHAMROCK SHAKE

Inspired by McDonald's

TOTAL TIME: 10 MIN · SERVES 2

Our cool, minty shake is even creamier and more delicious than the fast-food version sold at McDonald's in March, and you can make it all year round.

Shake

2½ cups vanilla ice cream

½ cup whole milk

¼ teaspoon mint extract

¼ teaspoon green food coloring

Toppings

whipped cream

sprinkles

maraschino cherries

1. Blend all shake ingredients in a blender until smooth.
2. Pour into a tall glass and top with whipped cream, sprinkles, and a maraschino cherry.

COPYCAT RASPBERRY DREAM

Inspired by Swig

TOTAL TIME: 5 MIN · SERVES 8

All you soda drinkers out there will *love* our version of Swig's Raspberry Dream soda. Dr Pepper, raspberries, coconut, and more create a dream of a drink!

2 cups fresh raspberries

½ cup sugar

2 cups half-and-half

2 tablespoons coconut extract

2 liters Dr Pepper, chilled

ice, for serving

1. In a blender, puree the raspberries and sugar together until smooth. Set aside.

2. In a small mixing bowl, combine the half-and-half and the coconut extract. Set aside.

3. Fill a 16-ounce cup halfway with ice. Then fill it three-fourths of the way with Dr Pepper. Add 2 tablespoons of the raspberry mixture, then 2 tablespoons of the cream mixture. Fill the rest of the cup with Dr Pepper, stir well with a straw or spoon, and enjoy!

NOTES

• The raspberry mixture will settle at the bottom, so you may have to stir the drink occasionally.

• We like to use Dr Pepper Ten, but diet, caffeine-free, and regular taste good too!

MINT JULEP

Inspired by Disneyland

PREP TIME: 5 MIN · COOK TIME: 10 MIN · CHILL TIME: 1 HOUR
TOTAL TIME: 1 HOUR AND 15 MIN · SERVES 10

Mint julep drinks are one of my favorite things to get at Disneyland. They are perfect for a hot summer day with a little bit of mint, lemon, and lime flavors. Mint juleps are often alcoholic, but the syrup used in this recipe is nonalcoholic.

Mint Julep

2 cups sugar

8 cups water

1 cup crème de menthe syrup

⅓ cup frozen lemonade concentrate

⅓ cup frozen limeade concentrate

a few drops of green food coloring (optional)

ice, for serving

Garnish

lemon wedges

mint sprigs

maraschino cherries

1. Add sugar and water to a large saucepan. Bring to a boil, stirring occasionally, then remove from heat. Cool for 5 minutes.

2. Pour the mixture into a large pitcher. Add the crème de menthe syrup and frozen lemonade and limeade concentrates. Add a little green food coloring and stir to mix.

3. Refrigerate until completely cooled, about 1 hour. Serve in a glass with some ice and garnish with lemon wedges, mint sprigs, and cherries.

HOMEMADE BUTTERBEER

Inspired by The Wizarding World of Harry Potter

TOTAL TIME: 10 MIN · SERVES 8

Our recipe tastes just like what they sell at The Wizarding World of Harry Potter. And this no-cook method is *so* easy!

Butterbeer

2 liters cream soda, chilled

¼ teaspoon caramel extract

¼ teaspoon butter extract

Butterscotch Cream Topping

1 cup heavy whipping cream

½ cup butterscotch topping

¼ cup powdered sugar

1. In a large pitcher, mix the cream soda with the caramel and butter extracts. Set aside.

2. In a large mixing bowl, use an electric mixer to whip heavy cream until it forms stiff peaks. Add butterscotch topping and powdered sugar. Mix to combine.

3. Pour the soda mixture into clear cups or mugs. Top with butterscotch cream topping and enjoy!

FROSTED LEMONADE

Inspired by Chick-fil-A

TOTAL TIME: 5 MIN · SERVES 2

Chick-fil-A's frosted lemonade is the perfect summertime treat. It's creamy, refreshing, and easy to make.

3 cups vanilla ice cream

1 cup Simply Lemonade

zest of 1 lemon (optional)

lemon slices, for garnish

1. Add ice cream, lemonade, and lemon zest to a blender and pulse until combined.

2. Pour into glasses and serve. Garnish with lemon slices, if desired.

DRINKS AND SHAKES

HOMEMADE FROSTY

Inspired by **Wendy's**

PREP TIME: 5 MIN · FREEZE TIME: 6 HOURS · TOTAL TIME: 6 HOURS 5 MIN · SERVES 4–6

Re-create this iconic, chocolaty treat in your own kitchen with only four ingredients!

1 (14-ounce) can sweetened condensed milk

1 (8-ounce container) Cool Whip, softened

8 cups milk

1 cup chocolate syrup

1. Mix sweetened condensed milk and Cool Whip in a large bowl until smooth.

2. Add milk and chocolate syrup and stir until combined. It will be runny.

3. Pour mixture into a large freezer-safe bowl or plastic pitcher. Freeze about 6 hours, stirring every hour, until it reaches preferred consistency.

NOTE

You can make this recipe up to a week ahead of time. There's no need to stir hourly. Just freeze in a freezer-safe container (or several smaller containers) with a lid. When you're ready to serve, remove from the freezer and allow to defrost at room temperature for about 20 minutes. Break into frozen chunks and blend in a blender until smooth.

PINK DRINK

Inspired by **Starbucks**

TOTAL TIME: 5 MIN · SERVES 2

Whip up a deliciously fruity Starbucks Pink Drink at home and re-create all that refreshing magic for a fraction of the cost.

6 large fresh strawberries, hulled

3 tablespoons sugar

¾ cup Ocean Spray White Cran-Strawberry juice

1 cup fresh coconut milk, divided

¼ cup freeze-dried strawberries, for topping

ice, for serving

1. Blend strawberries, sugar, and juice in a blender on high for 60 seconds.
2. Fill 2 (16-ounce) cups halfway with ice. Pour half of the strawberry mixture in each cup. Add ½ cup coconut milk to each cup and stir well. Top with freeze-dried strawberries.

NOTE

Use fresh coconut milk, not canned. You can find it in the refrigerator section near the milk.

RASPBERRY HOT CHOCOLATE WITH SOFT TOP

Inspired by Dutch Bros

TOTAL TIME: 5 MIN · SERVES 2

Indulge in the cozy goodness of Dutch Bros's raspberry hot chocolate—a delicious mix of smooth cocoa and lively raspberry flavor. It's topped off with a creamy soft layer, making it the perfect comforting winter drink.

4 cups chocolate milk

4 tablespoons Torani Raspberry Syrup

¼ cup Cool Whip, thawed

2 teaspoons sweetened condensed milk

1. In a microwave-safe bowl, combine chocolate milk and raspberry syrup. Microwave on high for 90 seconds, or until desired temperature. Pour into individual glasses.

2. In a small bowl, combine Cool Whip and sweetened condensed milk. Stir well and spoon over hot chocolate.

BREAKFAST

AVOCADO, BACON, AND EGG SANDWICH

Inspired by **Fork***, Boise, Idaho*

PREP TIME: 10 MIN · COOK TIME: 25 MIN · MARINATING TIME: 1 HOUR
TOTAL TIME: 1 HOUR 35 MIN · MAKES 4 SANDWICHES

This avocado, bacon, and egg sandwich is a copycat of our all-time favorite sandwich to get at a place in downtown Boise called Fork. It's called the BAM Sammy. Bacon. Avocado. Mozzarella. BAM.

½ cup pure maple syrup

¼ cup brown sugar

1 pound bacon

2 tomatoes

2 ripe avocados

4 eggs

8 slices bread

4 slices mozzarella cheese

½ cup fresh pesto

1. Mix together the maple syrup and brown sugar in a small bowl. Halve the bacon slices, make sure they are separated from each other, and place them all in a large plastic bag. Pour the syrup mixture over the bacon and seal. Place bag in the fridge to marinate for 1 hour.

2. Heat oven to 400 degrees F. After bacon has marinated, line a baking sheet with aluminum foil and top that with a wire rack. Arrange 6 small slices of bacon into a weave, repeating with remaining bacon, or you can cook the pieces normally. Bake for about 20 minutes, or until desired crispiness. Remove bacon but keep oven on.

3. While the bacon is cooking, slice the tomatoes and avocados. Cook the eggs over medium.

4. On another baking sheet, arrange the 8 slices of bread, 4 with sliced mozzarella cheese, 4 with a layer of pesto. Bake just until cheese begins to melt, about 5 minutes.

5. Arrange sandwiches with a slice of cheese bread topped with tomato, bacon, egg, and avocado, topped with a pesto slice.

NOTES

• Make sure your cooling rack is safe to use in the oven. Metal racks are fine, but if your rack has a nonstick coating, don't use it because it can warp.

• For the bread, we prefer sourdough, whole wheat, or croissants.

EGG BITES

Inspired by **Starbucks**

PREP TIME: 10 MIN · BAKE TIME: 20 MIN · TOTAL TIME: 30 MIN · MAKES 18 BITES

Discover the secrets to making Starbucks egg bites at home! With crispy bacon and creamy Gruyère cheese, they are a perfect on-the-go breakfast.

9 large eggs

1 cup cottage cheese

1¼ cup shredded Gruyère cheese

½ teaspoon salt

½ teaspoon pepper

½ teaspoon smoked paprika

½ cup finely chopped cooked bacon (about 6 slices)

1. Heat oven to 350 degrees F. Spray an 18-count muffin pan generously with nonstick cooking spray, or use muffin liners. Set aside.

2. Place eggs and cottage cheese in a blender and blend until smooth. Pour into a bowl and fold in cheese, salt, pepper, and paprika.

3. Fill each muffin cup about two-thirds full (with just under ¼ cup egg mixture). Top each egg bite with a rounded teaspoon of bacon. Gently press bacon into egg mixture.

4. Bake for 20–22 minutes, or until eggs are set. Remove and let sit for 5 minutes.

NOTE

If you're not using muffin liners, remove the egg bites from the tin using a plastic spoon.

COPYCAT EGG MCMUFFIN

Inspired by **McDonald's**

PREP TIME: 5 MIN · COOK TIME: 10 MIN · TOTAL TIME: 15 MIN · MAKES 1

These breakfast sandwiches are one of our favorite go-to morning meals. Make a bunch, freeze them, and have them on hand for busy mornings. Plus they taste just like the original!

1 English muffin

1 large egg

1 slice Canadian bacon or ham

1 slice American or cheddar cheese

1. Cut the English muffin in half, butter each side, and toast. You can toast it in the toaster, on a griddle, or in the oven at 300 degrees F. for a few minutes.

2. In a skillet, cook the egg to desired hardness.

3. In the same skillet, heat up the Canadian bacon or ham over medium heat until warm.

4. Assemble sandwich by layering the bottom half of the English muffin with cheese, egg, and Canadian bacon. Top with the other half of the toasted English muffin.

NOTES

• You can't go wrong making hash browns to serve alongside these sandwiches.

• To get that round egg shape that McDonald's is famous for, use a tuna can or a mason jar lid. Spray the inside with cooking spray and place it on a hot skillet. Break the egg into the can and poke the yolk. Cook it until it reaches the desired consistency, then slide the egg out. Perfect shape! You can also use an egg ring, an egg mold, or whatever you have on hand.

• Canadian bacon is the perfect round shape for this breakfast sandwich. Sometimes we'll use leftover dinner ham or even bacon slices. That's the beauty of making these breakfast sandwiches at home: you can make them however you want!

CHIA SEED PUDDING

Inspired by **The Stone Lizard**, *Blanding, Utah*

PREP TIME: 15 MIN · SET TIME: 3 HOURS · TOTAL TIME: 3 HOURS 15 MIN · SERVES 1

Chia seed pudding delivers a healthy dose of nutrition, including fiber, protein, and omega-3 fatty acids. It's great for breakfast, for a snack at home, or on the go!

½ cup milk

2 tablespoons chia seeds

1 teaspoon pure maple syrup

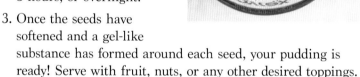

1. Combine the milk, chia seeds, and maple syrup in a bowl, cup, or reusable storage container. Stir well.

2. Let sit on the counter for 5–10 minutes. Stir again to make sure all the clumps are broken up. Cover and put in the fridge for at least 3 hours, or overnight.

3. Once the seeds have softened and a gel-like substance has formed around each seed, your pudding is ready! Serve with fruit, nuts, or any other desired toppings.

NOTE

Typically the ratio of ingredients is 2 tablespoons chia seeds and 1 teaspoon sweetener for every ½ cup liquid. If you want a thicker pudding, add more chia seeds. If you want a thinner pudding, add more liquid. You can also adjust the amount of sweetener to your taste.

CHILAQUILES

Inspired by **Liberty Market**, *Gilbert, Arizona*

PREP TIME: 10 MIN · COOK TIME: 20 MIN · TOTAL TIME: 30 MIN · SERVES 2

Easy chilaquiles are a popular Mexican breakfast that your family is going to love. This traditional dish includes fried corn tortillas, green salsa, fried eggs, and delicious toppings.

¼ cup canola oil, for frying

6 corn tortillas, quartered

10 ounces salsa verde or green enchilada sauce

2 eggs, fried or scrambled

1. Prepare a plate with a paper towel. Set aside.

2. In a large skillet, heat the oil over medium heat. Lightly fry each side of the tortilla quarters until they are golden brown and crispy, about 30–40 seconds. Place the fried chips on the paper towel to drain the oil.

3. Remove the oil from the skillet. In the skillet, heat the green sauce over medium heat until warm. Add tortilla chips and toss until all the chips are coated.

4. Add eggs and any additional toppings and serve immediately.

NOTE

Once you have the base of your easy chilaquiles, you can go crazy with toppings! This is such a fun breakfast to serve for special occasions. Just set up a topping bar and let your guests add anything they like. Yum! They're also delicious served with a side of refried beans. Here is a list of some topping ideas.

- avocado slices
- bacon
- black beans
- chipotles
- cilantro leaves
- cotija cheese
- diced green bell peppers
- diced tomatoes
- green chiles
- hot sauce
- lime juice
- lime wedges
- Mexican crema
- pickled red onions
- queso fresco
- radishes
- shredded cheese
- sour cream
- tomatillo salsa

PUMPKIN SPICE PANCAKES

Inspired by IHOP

PREP TIME: 5 MIN · COOK TIME: 15 MIN · TOTAL TIME: 20 MIN · SERVES 6

These pumpkin spice pancakes are a favorite pancake recipe for the fall season. It's like eating dessert for breakfast.

Pancakes

2 cups dry pancake mix

2 tablespoons brown sugar

1 teaspoon pumpkin pie spice

1½ cups water

½ cup pumpkin puree

Caramel Maple Syrup

1 cup brown sugar

1 cup heavy whipping cream

1 cup light corn syrup

½ teaspoon Crescent Mapleine imitation maple flavor

dash of ground cinnamon

Candied Pecans

½ cup chopped pecans

3 tablespoons brown sugar

dash of ground cinnamon

Pancakes

1. Heat a griddle or pan over medium heat. Coat with butter or nonstick cooking spray.

2. In a large bowl, combine pancake mix, brown sugar, and pumpkin pie spice. Whisk in water and pumpkin puree.

3. Pour about ½ cup batter for each pancake onto the warm griddle. Cook until bubbles appear on the top, then use a spatula to flip it onto the other side. Cook until golden brown on each side.

4. To serve, place pancakes on individual plates and top with syrup and candied pecans.

Caramel Maple Syrup

1. In a medium saucepan, combine all ingredients for the syrup. Cook over medium heat for 6–8 minutes, until the sugar completely dissolves.

Candied Pecans

1. In a small frying pan, cook the chopped pecans, brown sugar, and cinnamon over medium heat, stirring frequently, until the sugar melts and coats the pecans, about 3 minutes.

2. Immediately remove from heat and spread into a flat layer on a plate or baking sheet. Once completely cooled, you can break apart the candied pieces.

NOTES

- Use an ice-cream scoop to ladle the batter onto the griddle so the pancakes are all the same size.

- Keep pancakes warm by placing on a baking sheet, covering with foil, and keeping warm in the oven at 200 degrees F. until time to serve.

BREAKFAST BURRITO

Inspired by **The Chile Pepper**, *Yuma, Arizona*

PREP TIME: 15 MIN · COOK TIME: 15 MIN · TOTAL TIME: 30 MIN · MAKES 6

The Chile Pepper is a local, family-owned Mexican restaurant we discovered in Yuma, Arizona. They are famous for their breakfast burritos. Customize them by adding your favorite breakfast meats, cheeses, beans, and vegetables.

Breakfast Burrito

6 flour tortillas

8 eggs

½ cup milk

1 pound ham, sausage, or bacon, chopped

1⅓ cups shredded cheese (cheddar, Monterey Jack, pepper jack, or Mexican blend)

salt and pepper, to taste

More Fillings

2 cups hash browns or Tater Tots, cooked

2 cups refried beans, heated

1 cup mushrooms, sautéed

1 cup zucchini, sautéed

1 onion, finely diced and sautéed

2 Roma tomatoes, diced

1 bell pepper, diced

Toppings

1 avocado, sliced

1 cup guacamole

1 cup sour cream

1 cup salsa

1 cup diced fresh tomato

¼ cup fresh cilantro, chopped

1. Warm flour tortillas in oven or microwave. If using raw tortillas, prepare them according to package directions. Set aside.

2. Whisk eggs and milk together in a bowl. Set aside.

3. In a large skillet, cook preferred breakfast meat. If using diced ham, use a little oil or cooking spray in the pan before heating. Remove meat from the skillet and set aside.

4. In the same skillet, add egg mixture and stir until eggs are scrambled and cooked through. Add salt and pepper to taste.

5. Prepare your burritos by adding eggs, cheese, meat, and any other ingredients onto each tortilla. Roll each tortilla into a burrito and serve with toppings.

NOTES

• If you're going to add hash browns or vegetables, you can cook them in the same skillet as you cook the meat, before you cook the eggs. You can even retain a bit of the grease from cooking your sausage or bacon to cook your vegetables, hash browns, and eggs in. Otherwise, use cooking oil.

• To freeze, wrap each burrito in plastic wrap or foil. Place in a resealable plastic freezer bag or plastic container with a lid. Freeze up to 2 months.

- To reheat in microwave: Remove plastic wrap or foil and wrap burrito in a damp paper towel. Cook for 2–4 minutes on high, turning once.

- To reheat in an air fryer: Wrap the burrito in foil only. Reheat at 400 degrees F. for 15 minutes.

BREAKFAST PARFAITS

Inspired by McDonald's

TOTAL TIME: 15 MIN · SERVES 6

Make-ahead yogurt parfaits are a quick, healthy breakfast for busy mornings. Yogurt, granola, and fruit will start your day off right. Just grab and go!

32 ounces plain or vanilla yogurt

1½ cups sliced strawberries

1½ cups raspberries

1½ cups blueberries

4–5 cups granola

1. Mix berries together in a large bowl.
2. In 6 small cups or bowls, alternate layering mixed berries and yogurt until each cup is as full as you would like, with yogurt being the top layer.
3. Fill one snack-sized zip-top plastic bag for each cup with granola and seal.
4. Cover each cup tightly with plastic wrap and seal with a rubber band. Place a granola bag on each cup along with a plastic spoon. Place in refrigerator for up to 5 days.

NOTES

• Prepare for the week by making a double batch of these breakfast parfaits. Making them ahead of time is the best way to stay on track with meal planning and still have a delicious breakfast every morning.

• Greek yogurt works great for these parfaits.

• Find our recipe for homemade granola at favfamilyrecipes.com.

APPETIZERS AND SNACKS

SWEET CORN CAKES, OR TOMALITOS

Inspired by **Chevy's**

PREP TIME: 10 MIN · COOK TIME: 50 MIN · COOL TIME: 10 MIN
TOTAL TIME: 1 HOUR 10 MIN · SERVES 6

Sweet corn cakes, aka tomalitos, are a sweet yet savory side to any Mexican feast. They are creamy, they burst with flavor, and they're easy to make!

¼ cup butter, softened

¼ cup water

⅓ plus ¼ cup cornmeal, divided

1½ cups frozen whole-kernel corn, thawed

⅓ cup granulated sugar

2 tablespoons heavy whipping cream

¼ teaspoon salt

½ teaspoon baking powder

1. Heat oven to 350 degrees F. Prepare a water bath by filling a 9x13-inch baking dish one-third of the way with water. Set aside.

2. In a medium bowl, beat butter with a hand mixer until creamy. Add water and ⅓ cup cornmeal until well blended.

3. Using a food processor, process thawed corn, but leave it chunky. Stir into the butter mixture. Set aside.

4. In a separate bowl, mix remaining ¼ cup cornmeal, sugar, cream, salt, and baking powder. Add to the cornmeal mixture and stir to combine.

5. Pour batter into an ungreased 8x8-inch baking dish or casserole dish. Smooth the batter and cover the dish tightly with aluminum foil.

6. Place pan in prepared water bath. Bake for 50–60 minutes. Allow to cool for 10 minutes.

NOTES

• You can bake the tomalitos in 6 (10-ounce) custard cups instead of a baking dish if you want to create cute individual servings.

• The water bath helps the corn cake maintain moisture.

STICKY FINGERS WITH AMAZING SAUCE

Inspired by **Wingers**

PREP TIME: 10 MIN · COOK TIME: 20 MIN · TOTAL TIME: 30 MIN · SERVES 8

We make these Wingers Sticky Fingers and Amazing Sauce in less time than it would take to get take-out from Wingers. The sauce needs only *three* ingredients!

24 ounces frozen breaded chicken strips

Amazing Sauce

⅓ cup Frank's RedHot Original Sauce

1½ cups brown sugar

1 tablespoon water

1. Prepare chicken strips according to package directions. If you want to prepare them like Wingers does, deep-fry them. For a healthier method, bake or air-fry.

2. In a small saucepan, heat up all sauce ingredients until all the sugar dissolves, about 5 minutes.

3. Remove from heat and allow to cool to room temperature before adding to chicken strips.

NOTES

- For the chicken strips, we prefer Just Bare Lightly Breaded Chicken Breast Strips or Tyson Crispy Chicken Strips.
- The hot sauce has to be Frank's. No other sauce will taste as good.
- You can make the sauce ahead of time and keep it in the refrigerator. Warm it slightly in a saucepan until it thins enough to spread on the chicken.

COPYCAT BANG BANG SHRIMP

Inspired by Bonefish Grill

PREP TIME: 25 MIN · CHILL TIME: 20 MIN · COOK TIME: 3 MIN · TOTAL TIME: 48 MIN · SERVES 4

You are going to love this light and crispy copycat recipe from Bonefish Grill. The sauce is incredible. We love spicing it up with a little extra sriracha.

1 pound medium raw shrimp, peeled and deveined

8–12 cups vegetable oil, for frying

Spicy Sauce

½ cup mayonnaise

4 teaspoons sriracha sauce, or to taste

1 teaspoon sugar

1 teaspoon rice vinegar

Breading

½ cup flour

½ cup panko bread crumbs

1 teaspoon salt

½ teaspoon ground black pepper

¼ teaspoon onion powder

¼ teaspoon garlic powder

¼ teaspoon dried basil

Egg Mixture

1 egg, beaten

1 cup milk

1. Combine all spicy sauce ingredients in a small bowl. Cover and set aside.

2. Combine all breading ingredients in a shallow bowl. Set aside.

3. Combine beaten egg with milk in a shallow bowl. Set aside.

4. Bread the shrimp by dipping each in breading, then egg, then breading again. Arrange the coated shrimp on a plate and pop them into the fridge for at least 20 minutes. This step will help the breading to stick on the shrimp when they are frying.

5. Prepare a rack or a plate with paper towels to drain fried shrimp on. Set aside.

6. Heat oil in a deep fryer to 350 degrees F. Use the amount of oil required by your fryer. When oil is hot, fry shrimp 2–3 minutes each, or until golden brown. Drain on rack or prepared plate.

7. When all shrimp has been fried, place the shrimp in a large bowl. Spoon about ¼ cup sauce over shrimp and stir gently to coat.

NOTE

To bake your shrimp, heat oven to 350 degrees F. and line a baking sheet with aluminum foil. Bread shrimp and prepare sauce as described in the directions. Heat about ½ cup oil to 350 degrees F. in a skillet or frying pan. Fry shrimp on each side for 1–2 minutes, until coating is golden brown. Place on prepared baking sheet and bake for 8–10 minutes, until shrimp has turned pink.

FRIED BISCUITS

Inspired by **Carthay Circle Restaurant**, *Disney California Adventure Park*

PREP TIME: 10 MIN · COOK TIME: 6 MIN · FREEZE TIME: 6 HOURS
TOTAL TIME: 6 HOURS 16 MIN · MAKES 32 BISCUITS

These fried biscuits taste exactly like the spicy, cheesy biscuits found at Disney's California Adventure restaurant Carthay Circle. They are perfect little bites that are super easy to make at home!

1½ cups shredded Monterey Jack cheese

1½ cups shredded cheddar cheese

4–5 tablespoons finely diced jalapeño from a jar (not fresh)

5–6 slices cooked bacon, finely chopped

1 egg, beaten

1–2 teaspoons milk, or as needed

salt and pepper, to taste

1 (16.3-ounce) tube large biscuits (8 count)

oil, for frying

1. Cover a plate or tray with parchment paper. Set aside.

2. Combine cheeses, jalapeño, bacon, egg, milk, salt, and pepper in a medium mixing bowl. Mix with a spoon until well combined. It will keep its shape when you squeeze it together firmly in your hand.

3. Using a small cookie scoop, scoop a small ball (about the size of a typical bouncy ball) and roll it in your hands until it stays together and forms a smooth, tight ball. Repeat with remaining cheese mixture. You should have about 32 balls.

4. Place the balls on the prepared tray. Cover with plastic wrap. Freeze at least 6 hours or overnight.

5. Remove cheese balls from freezer.

6. Open the biscuit dough. Cut each biscuit into 4 sections. Flatten each section and wrap one around each cheese ball, rolling it in your hands to make sure there are no holes or seams. You want it to be smooth and round.

7. Heat oil in a deep fryer or skillet to 350 degrees F. Fry each ball until dark golden brown. Serve hot.

NOTES

• If the cheese inside doesn't seem to be completely melted, just pop them in the microwave for 10 seconds and they will be perfect.

• You can also serve them sweet with powdered sugar, cinnamon sugar, or honey butter. We like to mix our honey butter with a scoop of apricot jelly or strawberry jam.

JALAPEÑO CHEESE–FILLED PRETZELS

Inspired by **Disneyland**

PREP TIME: 20 MIN · COOK TIME: 10 MIN · RISE TIME: 1 HOUR
TOTAL TIME: 1 HOUR 30 MIN · MAKES 8 PRETZELS

The Jalapeño Cheese–Filled Pretzel is one of our very favorite treats at Disneyland. Now you can have this cheese-stuffed taste of Disney at home!

4 teaspoons active dry yeast

2 tablespoons sugar

1½ cups warm water

3 tablespoons oil

3¾ cups flour

1 teaspoon kosher salt

1 (1-pound) block jalapeño cheese or pepper jack cheese (not shredded)

⅓ cup baking soda

4 cups plus 1 tablespoon water, divided

1 egg

shredded cheese or coarse sea salt, for topping

1. In a small bowl, mix together yeast, sugar, and warm water. Let stand until foamy and creamy, about 10 minutes. Add oil to yeast mixture. Set aside.

2. In a stand mixer bowl or large bowl, combine flour and salt. Pour yeast mixture into flour mixture and knead on low speed for 10 minutes. (If mixing by hand, knead dough for same amount of time.)

3. Lightly oil a large bowl. Place dough inside, turning to coat. Cover with plastic wrap and let rise in a warm place for 1 hour, or until doubled in size.

4. While dough rises, cut cheese into 1-inch-long rectangular pieces. I did this by cutting the 1-pound block of cheese into fourths lengthwise, and then I cut each fourth in half lengthwise again to make 8 long sticks. (Each pretzel will use 1 of these long sticks of cheese.) Cut each stick into 1-inch-long pieces. Cover cheese to keep from drying out. Set aside.

5. When dough has risen, heat oven to 450 degrees F. Cover a baking sheet with aluminum foil and spray foil with cooking spray. Set aside.

6. Turn dough out onto a lightly floured surface and divide into 8 equal pieces. Roll each piece into a rope and use a rolling pin to flatten out.

7. Place cheese pieces along the middle of the dough, leaving a few inches of dough on each end without cheese. This will make it easier to twist into shape.

8. Pinch dough tightly up around the cheese and roll it out until it's in a rope shape again. Make sure there are no holes along the seam; you don't want the cheese to ooze out.

9. Twist into a pretzel shape. Cover with plastic wrap if needed to keep from drying out.

10. In a large saucepan, bring baking soda and 4 cups water to a boil, stirring until soda is dissolved. Remove from heat.

11. Completely dip each pretzel in the baking soda solution for 10-20 seconds each. Using a slotted spatula, remove pretzels from water and place on baking sheet. Pinch together any separated seams, if needed.

12. In a small bowl, beat egg with remaining 1 tablespoon water until foamy. Brush egg mixture over the top of each pretzel and sprinkle with cheese or sea salt.

13. Bake for 8-10 minutes, until golden brown.

SALSA

Inspired by Chili's

PREP TIME: 10 MIN · CHILL TIME: 2 HOURS · TOTAL TIME: 2 HOURS 10 MIN · MAKES 4 CUPS

With just the right balance of tanginess, heat, and freshness, this Chili's copycat recipe is sure to level up your chips and salsa game. You can add more diced jalapeños if you like it hot!

1 (14.5-ounce) can petite diced tomatoes

1 (10-ounce) can RO*TEL Diced Tomatoes & Green Chilies

2 teaspoons diced jalapeño peppers

½ small yellow onion, thickly sliced

1 teaspoon garlic powder

½ teaspoon sugar

1½ teaspoons salt

1 teaspoon cumin

1 teaspoon dried cilantro

2 teaspoons lime juice

1. Place all ingredients in a blender or food processor. Blend for 20 seconds or until desired chunkiness.

2. Pour into a quart jar, cover, and refrigerate at least 2 hours before serving.

QUESO

Inspired by Torchy's Tacos

PREP TIME: 10 MIN · COOK TIME: 10 MIN · TOTAL TIME: 20 MIN · SERVES 10

Bring the bold and cheesy flavor of Torchy's green chile queso to your own kitchen with our easy copycat recipe.

Queso

1 (16-ounce) container salsa verde

1 (4.5-ounce) container diced green chiles

1 pound Velveeta cheese, roughly cubed

⅓ cup heavy whipping cream

2 tablespoons Valentina hot sauce, plus more for serving

Garnish

cilantro

guacamole

cotija cheese

1. Place salsa verde, green chiles, and cheese cubes in a large pot. Heat over medium until the cheese melts. Then stir in heavy cream and hot sauce. Let simmer for a few minutes.

2. Serve with more hot sauce, cilantro, guacamole, and cotija cheese.

NOTES

• Store leftovers in an airtight container in the fridge.

• If your queso is a little thin, you can add about ⅓ cup shredded mild cheddar cheese to thicken it.

• Adjust the amount of hot sauce depending on how spicy you want your queso.

CRANBERRY JALAPEÑO DIP

Inspired by **Stonemill Kitchens, Costco**

TOTAL TIME: 10 MIN · SERVES 8

Tart cranberries combined with spicy jalapeños and mixed with sour lime juice create a favorite creamy cheesy dip that we all love to enjoy with crackers. It also makes a delicious spread for turkey or chicken sandwiches.

6 ounces fresh cranberries

1 jalapeño pepper, seeded and chopped

3 green onions, chopped

½ cup sugar

juice of 1 lime

16 ounces cream cheese, softened

½ cup sour cream

pinch of salt

1. Add the cranberries, jalapeño, green onion, sugar, and lime juice to a blender. Pulse or blend on low until just combined. You still want chunks of cranberry.

2. Pat some of the moisture off the cranberry mixture and then add it to a mixing bowl. Add the cream cheese, sour cream, and salt. Mix with a stand mixer or hand mixer until everything is fully incorporated.

3. Serve with celery sticks, cucumber slices, tortilla chips, pita chips, RITZ crackers, Wheat Thins, sliced bell peppers, or pretzels.

NOTES

• Roughly chop the jalapeño and green onions before blending to ensure consistently sized chunks. For a less spicy dip, be sure to remove all the seeds and ribs from the jalapeño before blending.

• Store leftovers in the fridge in an airtight container.

CRISP BEAN BURRITO

Inspired by Taco Time

PREP TIME: 10 MIN · COOK TIME: 5 MIN · TOTAL TIME: 15 MIN · SERVES 5

This crisp bean burrito is a delicious snack or a quick lunch that's packed with protein. Enjoy a bean burrito fried or baked—either way, you'll love this simple, tasty recipe.

½ cup oil

5 soft flour tortillas

1 cup refried beans

¼ cup shredded cheese, or to taste

1. Heat oven to 400 degrees F. Set aside a baking sheet.

2. Heat oil in a medium-sized skillet. Spread about 3 tablespoons refried beans on each tortilla, sprinkle with cheese, then roll up. Fry in oil for 15–30 seconds on each side.

3. Place burritos on baking sheet and bake for 5–7 minutes.

4. Remove from oven and serve. Dip in enchilada sauce, guacamole, sour cream, or salsa.

NOTE

Be as creative as you would like. Add all sorts of ingredients from shredded meat to vegetables into your fried burrito. Feel free to create your own little salsa bar at home with your favorite toppings and find out what you like dipping them in the best! We love dipping them in ranch dressing and guacamole. Kick it up a notch, too! Spoon a thin layer of hot sauce over the crisp bean burritos for a spicy variation.

GUACAMOLE

Inspired by **Barbacoa Mexican Grill**

TOTAL TIME: 15 MIN · SERVES 8

This truly is the best guacamole *ever*. It's the only guacamole recipe you'll ever need. Grab yourself a few fresh ingredients and you've got yourself the best guac in town!

3 avocados

¼ cup finely diced red onion

2 cloves garlic, minced

½ bunch cilantro leaves, chopped

1 jalapeño, finely chopped

1 large tomato or 2 small tomatoes, diced

1 lime, juiced

4–5 shakes green Tabasco sauce

kosher salt, to taste

fresh cracked black pepper, to taste

1. Pit avocados and place in a bowl. If you like your guac chunky, coarsely chop the avocados. If you like your guac smooth, mash them instead.

2. Add the rest of the ingredients to the bowl. Stir until all the ingredients are distributed evenly.

LETTUCE WRAPS

Inspired by **P.F. Chang's**

PREP TIME: 10 MIN · COOK TIME: 15 MIN · TOTAL TIME: 25 MIN · SERVES 6

Our copycat Asian lettuce wraps are packed with fresh ingredients and vibrant flavors. The dipping sauces are a must! Be sure to try both the creamy and spicy versions.

1 head butter lettuce, leaves separated

Teriyaki Sauce

1 cup teriyaki sauce

⅓ cup sweet chili sauce

¼ cup soy sauce

1 tablespoon finely minced or grated fresh ginger

red pepper flakes, to taste

Chicken Filling

4 tablespoons oil, divided

1 ½ pounds boneless skinless chicken breast, diced into small pieces

salt and pepper, to taste

½ cup sliced green onion

2 cloves garlic, minced

½ cup chopped water chestnuts

½ cup pine nuts or cashews, chopped

⅓ cup chopped mushroom (optional)

Dipping Sauces

remaining teriyaki sauce (about ⅔–¾ cup)

¼ teaspoon sriracha sauce, or to taste

1–2 tablespoons creamy peanut butter

Teriyaki Sauce

1. Combine all teriyaki sauce ingredients in a bowl. Mix well and set aside.

Chicken Filling

1. In a large skillet, heat 2 tablespoons oil over medium heat. Season chicken lightly with salt and pepper. When oil is hot, add chicken. Cook until chicken is white on all sides (it doesn't need to be completely cooked through), then remove chicken from skillet and set aside on a plate. Discard any extra juices.

2. In the same skillet, heat remaining 2 tablespoons oil over medium-high heat. Add onion, garlic, water chestnuts, pine nuts or cashews, and mushrooms. Sauté for 1–2 minutes.

3. Add chicken and about half of the teriyaki mixture to the skillet. Cook for 7–8 minutes, stirring often, until chicken is cooked through.

4. Place 2–3 tablespoons of the chicken mixture in the center of each lettuce leaf, roll up, and enjoy!

Dipping Sauces

1. Heat remaining teriyaki sauce in a small saucepan. Simmer for about 5 minutes. Remove from heat.

2. Divide sauce into 2 small bowls.

3. In one bowl, add sriracha sauce and mix well. In the other bowl, add creamy peanut butter and mix until smooth.

NOTE

Half of the teriyaki mixture will be used in the chicken filling, and the other half will be used to make the dipping sauces. For the ingredients, we like Mr. Yoshida's original teriyaki sauce and the Mae Ploy brand of sweet chili sauce.

LUNCHTIME

ZUPPA TOSCANA

Inspired by Olive Garden

PREP TIME: 20 MIN · COOK TIME: 4 HOURS · TOTAL TIME: 4 HOURS 20 MIN · SERVES 8

In our opinion, this Zuppa Toscana copycat recipe is actually better than the original from Olive Garden! It has a creamy broth base and is loaded with sausage and potatoes.

1 pound Johnsonville mild ground Italian sausage

5¼ cups (42 ounces) chicken broth

2 cups heavy whipping cream

red pepper flakes, to taste

salt and pepper, to taste

½ pound bacon, cooked and crumbled

4 cups kale, chopped

3 medium potatoes, scrubbed, halved, and thinly sliced

1. Heat a frying pan over medium-high heat. Form the sausage into little balls. Brown the sausage in the frying pan, stirring frequently. Remove to a plate lined with paper towels to drain off some of the grease.

2. Put everything except for the potatoes together in a large slow cooker. Cook on high for 3–4 hours. If you prefer your kale more crisp-tender, wait to add the kale with the potatoes. Add potatoes during the last 40–60 minutes of cooking.

3. Stir well and serve with breadsticks and salad.

NOTES

• Instead of breaking off small pieces of sausage and rolling them in your hands, simply cut the sausage using a knife in a crisscross pattern. The sausage will roll up into balls as you cook and stir it in the skillet. Break it up into more bite-size pieces with your spatula or spoon if needed.

• You can really use any kind of potato you want in this recipe. Russet potatoes work great, but you can also use a waxy potato like a Yukon Gold or red potato. You can leave the skins on, or you can peel them. Totally up to you.

• Prepackaged, pre-rinsed kale will make your life easier. You can also get kale from the produce department. Just make sure you rinse it *really* well.

TORTILLA SOUP

Inspired by Cafe Rio

PREP TIME: 15 MIN · COOK TIME: 20 MIN · SIMMER TIME: 30 MIN
TOTAL TIME: 1 HOUR 5 MIN · SERVES 6

If you love Cafe Rio's tortilla soup but don't want to go out, don't worry! We've got you covered with this *amazing* copycat recipe.

Soup

1 onion, diced

1 tablespoon vegetable oil

½ teaspoon cumin

¼ teaspoon cayenne pepper, plus more to taste

½ teaspoon chili powder

5 cups (40 ounces) chicken broth

3 tablespoons finely chopped fresh cilantro

½ lime, juiced

1 (15.5-ounce) can pinto beans, drained and rinsed

pepper, to taste

Chicken

2 tablespoons taco seasoning

1 tablespoon paprika

oil, for brushing

2 boneless skinless chicken breasts

Toppings

pico de gallo

2 avocados, diced

2 cups pepper jack cheese

tortilla strips

cilantro

lime wedges

1. In a small skillet, sauté onion in oil until onion becomes slightly soft. Stir in cumin, cayenne, and chili powder. Sauté an additional 1–2 minutes.

2. Transfer seasoned onions to a large pot or saucepan. Add chicken broth, cilantro, lime juice, pinto beans, and pepper. Bring to a boil over medium-high heat, then simmer on low heat for at least 30 minutes.

3. In the meantime, when you are close to serving, combine taco seasoning and paprika. Brush chicken with oil and rub with seasoning mixture. Grill chicken over medium heat until cooked through. (Try to turn only once during the grilling process.) Remove from grill and shred.

4. In small individual bowls, layer chicken, a few tablespoons pico de gallo, ⅓ cup diced avocado, and ⅓ cup pepper jack cheese. Ladle about 1 ½ cups broth directly over the layers. Top with tortilla strips and garnish with cilantro and lime wedges.

NOTES

• You can cook this soup in a slow cooker instead of simmering it on the stove. Put the sautéed onions and the remaining soup ingredients in a medium-sized slow cooker on low for at least 2–3 hours. You can throw the chicken in the slow cooker with the broth and it will taste rich and delicious, but personally we *love* the smoky grilled chicken taste. Grill it if you can!

• We added pinto beans to this recipe. It's not the Cafe Rio original way of doing things, but it is totally worth doing. The meaty beans give it a deeper flavor and actually make the soup go further. If you want to keep it *exactly* like Cafe Rio, feel free to leave them out.

• Instead of adding a scoop of guacamole like Cafe Rio does, add diced avocado, which saves the time of having to make a separate little thing of guacamole. Plus the chunks of cool avocado are delicious.

PASTA E FAGIOLI SOUP

Inspired by Olive Garden

PREP TIME: 15 MIN · COOK TIME: 8 HOURS · TOTAL TIME: 8 HOURS 15 MIN · SERVES 20

This copycat recipe of Olive Garden's pasta e fagioli soup tastes just like the original. It's a hearty, Italian-seasoned soup and is easily made in a slow cooker.

2 pounds ground beef

1 onion, chopped

1 cup shredded carrots

1 cup chopped celery

1 (28-ounce) can diced tomatoes, undrained

1 (16-ounce) can red kidney beans, drained

1 (16-ounce) can white kidney beans, drained

4 cups beef stock

1 tablespoon dried oregano

2 teaspoons salt

2 teaspoons pepper

1½ tablespoons dried parsley, plus more for garnish

1 teaspoon Tabasco sauce

1 (24-ounce) bottle Prego Traditional pasta sauce

8 ounces ditalini pasta

Parmesan cheese, for serving

1. Brown ground beef in large skillet. Drain fat.
2. Add beef and all ingredients except the pasta and Parmesan cheese into a large slow cooker. Cook on low for 7–8 hours or high for 4–5 hours.
3. Before serving, cook pasta according to package directions. Drain and add to soup.
4. Serve in bowls topped with Parmesan cheese and parsley, if desired.

NOTE

We love to serve this soup with crusty bread, breadsticks, or corn bread.

CHICKEN ENCHILADA CHILI

Inspired by Café Zupas

PREP TIME: 10 MIN · COOK TIME: 4 HOURS · TOTAL TIME: 4 HOURS 10 MIN · SERVES 6

You have got to try our slow-cooker version of Café Zupas's chicken enchilada chili! It's loaded with seasoned chicken, beans, and corn in a creamy, slightly spicy soup.

Soup

2 boneless skinless chicken breasts

2 cups red enchilada sauce

1 cup green enchilada sauce

1 (22.6-ounce) can cream of chicken soup

1 cup milk

1 (10-ounce) can RO*TEL Diced Tomatoes & Green Chilies

2 tablespoons chili powder

1 teaspoon paprika

1 teaspoon salt

1 (15-ounce) can black beans, drained and rinsed

1 (15-ounce) can corn, drained

1 cup shredded cheddar cheese

½ cup sour cream

Toppings

tortilla strips

sour cream

shredded cheddar cheese

fresh lime juice

cilantro

sliced avocado

1. In a large slow cooker, add the chicken breasts and both kinds of enchilada sauce. Cook for approximately 3 hours on high, until the chicken is cooked and will shred into the sauce.

2. After shredding the chicken, add all remaining soup ingredients except the sour cream. Cook for 1 more hour.

3. Turn off the heat. Whisk in the sour cream. Serve in individual bowls and garnish with toppings of choice.

NOTES

• You can use our homemade red enchilada sauce in this recipe—it makes the soup especially good. Find it at favfamilyrecipes.com.

• Check the expiration date on dry spices and seasonings. Make sure they are fresh so they will give flavor to the chili.

• If you don't have time for the slow cooker, you can make this recipe on the stovetop with an easy shortcut. Buy a rotisserie chicken at your local grocery store and shred the meat. Add it to a large pot on the stovetop along with the enchilada sauces. Bring to a boil. Add remaining ingredients except the sour cream and simmer, covered, for 30 minutes. Stir in sour cream and serve.

TOMATO BASIL SOUP

Inspired by Café Zupas

PREP TIME: 10 MIN · COOK TIME: 35 MIN · TOTAL TIME: 45 MIN · SERVES 8

This creamy tomato basil soup inspired by Café Zupas is one of our very favorite soups. It is simple to make and is so rich and creamy!

4 tablespoons butter

1 medium onion, chopped

1 carrot, chopped

1 rib celery, chopped

3 cloves garlic, minced

1 tablespoon flour

1 cup chicken broth

3 (14.5-ounce) cans stewed tomatoes, or about 5–6 cups diced tomatoes

⅔ cup pesto

1 teaspoon dried oregano

1 teaspoon brown sugar

1 cup heavy whipping cream

salt and pepper, to taste

fresh grated Parmesan cheese, for garnish

fresh basil, for garnish

cooked orzo pasta, for garnish

1. In a large soup pot, melt butter over medium heat. Add onion, carrot, celery, and garlic. Sauté until veggies become soft and clear.

2. Stir in the flour and cook for about 2 minutes. Pour in chicken broth, whisking constantly. Add tomatoes and bring to a boil, stirring often.

3. Stir in pesto, oregano, and brown sugar. Reduce heat to low. Simmer for 30 minutes.

4. Remove from heat and cool for 15 minutes. Blend in a blender, working in batches, or using an immersion blender until smooth.

5. Return to pot and heat over medium until warm. Whisk in heavy cream and add salt and pepper to taste.

6. Garnish with Parmesan cheese, basil, and orzo and serve.

NOTES

• If using a slow cooker, the instructions are nearly the same except that instead of simmering for 30 minutes, transfer the soup to the slow cooker and cook on low for at least 4 hours.

• Store soup in an airtight container in the refrigerator for up to 5 days. When ready to reheat, place in the microwave or cook on medium-low heat until it is warmed through.

• Here are some ideas for variations on this recipe:

  - Use fresh basil leaves, garlic powder, or onion powder to add flavor. Add red pepper flakes, paprika, or chili powder for more spice.

  - In place of butter, you can cook your vegetables in olive oil or canola oil.

  - For a healthier version, replace heavy cream with coconut or almond milk.

CHILI

Inspired by **Wendy's**

PREP TIME: 10 MIN · COOK TIME: 15 MIN · SIMMER TIME: 2–3 HOURS
TOTAL TIME: 3 HOURS AND 25 MIN · SERVES 6–8

This copycat recipe brings the iconic flavors of Wendy's chili to your kitchen. With this recipe you can discover the secrets behind this ultimate comfort food.

2½ pounds ground beef

1 cup diced celery

2 cups diced white onion

1 large green bell pepper, diced

1 tablespoon minced garlic

1 cup water

1 cup tomato juice

1 (28-ounce) can stewed tomatoes

1 (10-ounce) can RO*TEL Diced Tomatoes & Green Chilies

1½ (1.25-ounce) packets McCormick Mild Chili Seasoning Mix

1 (14-ounce) can red kidney beans, undrained

1 (15-ounce) can Ranch Style Original Beans, undrained

1 teaspoon salt

½ teaspoon pepper

1. In a large pot, brown beef. Drain off excess fat.

2. Add celery, onion, green bell pepper, and garlic. Cook on medium-high for 3–5 minutes, until vegetables are softened.

3. Add all remaining ingredients. Cover and simmer for 2–3 hours, stirring occasionally, until it reaches desired thickness.

FUJI APPLE SALAD

Inspired by Panera Bread

PREP TIME: 15 MIN · CHILL TIME: 30 MIN · TOTAL TIME: 45 MIN · SERVES 6

Enjoy the freshness of Panera Bread's famous Fuji apple salad with this easy-to-follow copycat recipe. Crisp mixed greens, juicy apple slices, grilled chicken, and an apple vinaigrette create a delightful salad that can be served as a side or a main dish.

Salad

6 cups chopped romaine lettuce

2 cups baby arugula

2 cups sliced grilled chicken

⅓ small red onion, thinly sliced

1 cup pecan halves

1¾ cups dehydrated apple slices (crispy, not soft)

¾ cup crumbled Gorgonzola cheese

2 Roma tomatoes

Dressing

½ cup olive oil

¼ cup white wine vinegar

½ cup honey

3 tablespoons 100% apple juice (not from concentrate)

½ teaspoon salt

⅓ teaspoon onion powder

¼ teaspoon garlic powder

1. Place salad dressing ingredients in a blender. Blend for 30 seconds. Pour into a glass jar and refrigerate for at least 30 minutes.

2. Assemble all salad ingredients in a large bowl.

3. Pour dressing over the salad and toss, or serve on the side.

NUTS ABOUT BERRIES SALAD

Inspired by Café Zupas

TOTAL TIME: 15 MIN · MAKES 8 SIDE DISH SALADS OR 4 MAIN DISH SALADS

This Nuts about Berries copycat salad is colorful, flavorful, and refreshing in the spring and summer months when you can pick or purchase delicious fresh berries.

Salad

8 cups spinach and spring salad mix

1 cup raspberries

1 cup strawberries

1 cup blackberries

1 cup blueberries

⅛ cup feta cheese

Raspberry Vinaigrette

¼ cup white wine vinegar

½ cup raspberries

1½ tablespoons honey

1½ tablespoons olive oil

¼ teaspoon salt

dash of fresh ground pepper

Cinnamon Pecans

½ cup coarsely chopped pecans

1 tablespoon sugar

2 teaspoons cinnamon

Salad

1. Wash and dry the berries.
2. Place salad mix in a large bowl. Toss berries, feta cheese, and cinnamon pecans over the greens. Top with raspberry vinaigrette.

Raspberry Vinaigrette

1. Place all ingredients in a blender and blend until smooth.

Cinnamon Pecans

1. Heat pecans and sugar in a skillet over medium heat. Stir constantly until the sugar has just melted. Sprinkle cinnamon over pecans.
2. Immediately place pecans on a piece of aluminum foil to cool. The pecans will burn if they are left in the skillet.

NOTES

• Candied almonds or pecans can be used in place of the cinnamon pecans.

• Goat cheese or blue cheese can be used in place of the feta cheese.

• Red onion can be added for a boost of flavor.

• Poppy seed dressing, balsamic vinegar dressing, our homemade creamy Strawberry Vinaigrette (available at favfamilyrecipes .com), or a store-bought raspberry vinaigrette can be used in place of the homemade dressing.

COPYCAT OLIVE GARDEN SALAD WITH OG DRESSING

Inspired by Olive Garden

PREP TIME: 15 MIN · CHILL TIME: 30 MIN · TOTAL TIME: 45 MIN · SERVES 6

Create a replica of Olive Garden's renowned garden-fresh salad in your own kitchen. Crisp lettuce, ripe tomatoes, black olives, and zesty croutons, all drizzled with the signature Italian dressing, make for one superb salad.

Salad

2 small heads romaine lettuce, chopped

½ small red onion, sliced

2 Roma tomatoes, sliced

3 ounces (about ½ cup) medium black olives, drained

4 whole pepperoncini peppers

⅓ cup grated Parmesan cheese

1–2 cups Texas Toast Seasoned Croutons

Dressing

⅔ cup high-quality extra-virgin olive oil

1 (7-ounce) package Good Seasons Italian Dressing Mix

⅓ cup white wine vinegar

¼ cup water

1 tablespoon light corn syrup

2 tablespoons mayonnaise

¾ teaspoon Dijon mustard

½ teaspoon garlic powder

¼ cup grated Parmesan cheese

1. Place all dressing ingredients in a blender and mix until well combined. Pour into a jar, cover, and refrigerate for at least 30 minutes.

2. Arrange salad ingredients in a large bowl. Add dressing until well coated, or serve dressing on the side.

ORIENTAL CHICKEN SALAD

Inspired by Applebee's

PREP TIME: 20 MIN · COOK TIME: 6 MIN · TOTAL TIME: 26 MIN · MAKES 6 DINNER SALADS

This copycat recipe of Applebee's Oriental Chicken Salad tastes just like the popular restaurant dish! Crisp veggies, chow mein, and tender chicken taste divine in that creamy signature dressing.

Dressing

½ cup mayonnaise

6 tablespoons honey

3 tablespoons rice vinegar

1 tablespoon Dijon mustard

½ teaspoon toasted sesame oil

¼ teaspoon salt

Chicken Strips

2 cups vegetable oil, for frying

1 egg

¾ cup buttermilk

¾ cup flour

½ cup cornflake crumbs

½ cup panko bread crumbs

2 teaspoons salt

¼ teaspoon pepper

3 boneless skinless chicken breasts

Salad

6 cups chopped romaine lettuce

1 cup chopped red cabbage

¾ cup julienned or shredded carrots

½ cup sliced almonds

1 cup chow mein noodles

Dressing

1. Thoroughly mix dressing ingredients. Chill until ready to serve.

Chicken Strips

1. Fill a deep frying pan with about 2 inches of oil. Heat to 350 degrees F. Prepare a rack or plate with a paper towel for draining fried chicken. Set aside.

2. Whisk egg and buttermilk together in a small bowl. Set aside.

3. In a separate bowl, stir flour, cornflakes, bread crumbs, salt, and pepper together. Set aside.

4. Use a mallet or rolling pin to pound each chicken breast evenly to about a 1-inch thickness. This is easiest if you place each chicken breast between two sheets of waxed paper or plastic wrap before flattening. Slice each chicken breast lengthwise into 4 or 5 strips.

5. Dredge each chicken strip in egg mixture, then dry crumb mixture. Place each strip in heated oil and fry for 6–7 minutes, or until golden brown. Remove to rack or prepared plate.

Salad

1. Prepare salad by tossing romaine with red cabbage and carrots. Evenly distribute salad to 6 dinner plates.

2. Slice the chicken strips diagonally into thirds, or leave in strips. Top each salad with hot chicken strips.

3. Garnish each salad with almonds and chow mein noodles. Serve with dressing on the side.

NOTE

We like to caramelize the almonds in a saucepan with 2 tablespoons sugar.

WALDORF SALAD

Inspired by Waldorf Astoria Hotel

TOTAL TIME: 15 MIN · SERVES 12

Waldorf salad is fresh, crisp, crunchy, and sweet. So refreshing and filling, it's the perfect side dish to any meal!

3 Fuji, Gala, or Pink Lady apples, chopped

3 Granny Smith apples, chopped

1 tablespoon lemon juice

1 cup chopped celery (about 3 ribs)

2 cups red grapes, halved

1 cup walnuts, halved

¾ cup mayonnaise or plain yogurt

3 cups green leaf lettuce or mixed salad greens

1. Place apple chunks in a bowl and toss in lemon juice. Mix celery, grapes, and walnuts in with the apples. Add mayonnaise or yogurt and stir until the fruit and nuts are well coated.

2. Refrigerate salad until ready to serve. Serve on a bed of green leaf lettuce or mixed salad greens.

RONTO WRAPS

Inspired by **Ronto Roasters**, *Star Wars: Galaxy's Edge, Disneyland*

PREP TIME: 20 MIN · COOK TIME: 1 HOUR 15 MIN · REST TIME: 1 HOUR
TOTAL TIME: 2 HOURS 35 MIN · SERVES 6

Ronto wraps are a gyro-style entrée made with pork sausage and sliced pork in a soft pita, topped with tangy slaw and a creamy peppercorn dressing. If you haven't tried it yet, it is a *must* on your next Disney vacation. These wraps can be found in Star Wars: Galaxy's Edge at both Walt Disney World Resort and the Disneyland Resort. In the meantime, you can make your own using our easy copycat recipe!

6 grilled pork sausages or hot dogs

6 flatbread pitas (no pockets)

Peppercorn Sauce

1 cup mayonnaise

¼ cup water

¼ cup fresh lemon juice

¼ teaspoon ground cardamom

⅛ teaspoon ground sumac

kosher salt, to taste

freshly ground black peppercorns, to taste

Pork Roast

2 pounds pork roast or pork loin

1 tablespoon olive oil

1 tablespoon dry ranch seasoning

½ teaspoon garlic powder

½ teaspoon salt

¼ teaspoon paprika

Tangy Slaw

3 cups tricolor coleslaw mix

3 tablespoons olive oil

3 tablespoons apple cider vinegar or distilled white vinegar

1 teaspoon sugar (optional)

kosher salt, to taste

pepper, to taste

Peppercorn Sauce

1. Combine all ingredients in a small bowl and whisk until smooth.

2. Cover and refrigerate at least 1 hour or until ready to serve. The longer it rests, the better. Overnight is best.

Pork Roast

1. Preheat oven to 425 degrees F. Remove roast from the refrigerator and allow to come to room temperature, about 30 minutes. Pat pork dry and rub with olive oil.

2. In a small bowl, combine ranch powder, garlic powder, salt, and paprika. Rub evenly over the roast.

3. Place roast in a glass baking dish or oven-safe ceramic Dutch oven. Bake for 15 minutes.

4. Reduce oven heat to 350 degrees F. Bake for another 30 minutes, or until internal temperature reaches 145 degrees F.

5. Remove from the oven, wrap in foil, and allow to rest 15–20 minutes before slicing. Cut into thin slices immediately before serving.

Tangy Slaw

1. Place cabbage slaw in a medium bowl. In a small bowl whisk together oil, vinegar, sugar, salt, and pepper until well combined. Toss with cabbage slaw until slaw is well coated with dressing. Cover and refrigerate until ready to serve.

Assembly

1. Grill smoked sausages until completely cooked through and slightly charred on the outside, about 10 minutes on each side or until internal temperature is 160 degrees F.

2. Soften the pita bread by warming it for a few seconds on a hot grill, or microwave for 10 seconds. Place about ½ cup

sliced pork on each pita. Place the grilled smoked sausage over the middle and top with slaw and peppercorn sauce.

NOTES

- Start with the peppercorn sauce so the flavors have time to bloom while you are preparing the other ingredients. You can find ground sumac in a small packet at any Asian market. If necessary, it can be left out of the peppercorn dressing.

- When cooking the roast, always use a meat thermometer to determine doneness. If you have a larger roast, plan on your roasting time being an additional 15–20 minutes per pound after the initial 15 minutes. So if you have a 3-pound roast, the cook time will be closer to 45–60 minutes. If you are roasting a pork loin or tenderloin, you will need less time since it is thinner. Check the temperature after 15 minutes and continue checking until the internal temp is 145 degrees F.

- If you keep the roast covered and wait to slice it until you're ready to serve, that will help prevent the pork from drying out.

- You can make your own cabbage and carrot slaw mix to replace the store-bought tricolor mix by combining 2½ cups chopped cabbage and ½ cup matchstick carrots.

HOMEMADE FOOTLONG BREAD

Inspired by **Subway**

PREP TIME: 2 HOURS 20 MIN · BAKE TIME: 25 MIN
TOTAL TIME: 2 HOURS 45 MIN · MAKES 3 (12-INCH) LOAVES

This bread recipe is so easy to make and tastes even better than the popular restaurant's version. Soft and chewy, it's the perfect start to your favorite sandwich!

2 tablespoons active dry yeast

1½ cups warm water, divided

2 tablespoons sugar

3½ cups flour

2 tablespoons Bob's Red Mill Vital Wheat Gluten

3 tablespoons butter, cold, plus a little more for topping

½ tablespoon salt

1. In the bowl of a stand mixer fitted with a dough hook, combine yeast, ½ cup warm water, and sugar. Stir until well combined. Let stand for about 10 minutes, or until nice and foamy.

2. In a separate mixing bowl, combine flour and vital wheat gluten. Set aside.

3. Add remaining 1 cup warm water to the yeast mixture. Add the flour mixture. Mix until combined, about 4 minutes. Add a little flour if necessary; you want it a little sticky, but not so much that it sticks to the sides of the bowl.

4. Cut up cold butter into little cubes and add to the mixing bowl. Add salt. Mix an additional 5-6 minutes, until butter is mixed in. Pull the bread off the hook if needed throughout the mixing process. Again, you want the dough to be slightly sticky and stretchy.

5. Grease a large bowl. Place dough inside and roll around a little to get it greased all around. Cover and allow to rise in a warm place for about 1 hour.

6. Punch dough down and divide into 3 equal pieces. (Flour your hands if the dough is too sticky, for easier handling.) Roll out each piece into a 12-inch-long loaf. The dough should be the same thickness all the way across. Place on a nonstick baking sheet, a baking sheet with a silicone baking mat, or a French bread baking pan. Cover and allow to rise 40–60 minutes, until dough doubles in size.

7. Heat oven to 350 degrees F. Bake for 15–25 minutes (check at 15 minutes), until bread is golden brown. Remove from oven and lightly run a little cold butter over the top.

8. Allow loaves to cool completely, then serve with all your favorite sub sandwich toppings!

NOTES

- You can make variations of this bread easily. To make whole wheat bread, use whole wheat flour. You can also add sesame seeds and a drizzle of olive oil to the top of your bread before baking. For Italian bread or Italian herb bread, sprinkle Italian seasoning or some oregano on the top of your loaf before baking. You can make cheese bread by sprinkling shredded Parmesan cheese on the top of the loaves before baking.

- If you use a bread mold, you'll get the perfect shape each time.

SLIDERS

Inspired by **White Castle**

PREP TIME: 10 MIN · COOK TIME: 40 MIN · TOTAL TIME: 50 MIN · MAKES 12 SLIDERS

You can make this version of White Castle sliders yourself at home! If you've always wanted to replicate these popular burgers, this recipe is the real deal.

2 pounds ground beef

1 (2-ounce) packet Lipton onion soup mix

1 tablespoon peanut butter

½ cup milk

1 onion, finely chopped

12 cheese slices

12 slider rolls

1. Heat oven to 350 degrees F. Set aside a baking sheet.

2. In a large bowl, mix together the ground beef, Lipton onion soup mix, peanut butter, and milk. Spread the meat mixture on the baking sheet. Use a rolling pin to roll over the meat to smooth it out. Bake for about 10 minutes. The meat will shrink.

3. Put the diced onion all around the edges. Bake another 15 minutes.

4. Spoon the onion from the edges all over the top of the meat. Layer with cheese slices. Bake another 7–10 minutes, until cheese is melted.

5. Add the tops of the rolls (the bottom part of the rolls will just sit on the counter). Bake for about 5 more minutes.

6. Remove from oven. Slice the meat into individual sliders with a pizza cutter. Pick up the slider meat and its top bun with a spatula and set it on the bottom bun.

NOTES

- You can find slider rolls in the bakery section of the grocery store. You may be able to fit more or fewer buns on the meat, depending on the size of the buns.

- Once you have your cheese sliders baked and cut, you can top them with all kinds of toppings: ketchup, mustard, mayonnaise, or other condiments; dill pickle slices (you'll probably want 20–24 dill pickle chips for these, especially if you're a fan of dill pickles); lime pickles; garlic powder; and a pinch of salt.

SOUTHERN FRIED CHICKEN SANDWICH

Inspired by Donnie Mac's

PREP TIME: 25 MIN · CHILL TIME: OVERNIGHT · COOK TIME: 15 MIN
TOTAL TIME: 40 MIN PLUS OVERNIGHT · SERVES 4

This Southern fried chicken sandwich is light and crispy on the outside, juicy and flavorful on the inside, and topped with a crunchy corn slaw. It's hearty and delicious! This recipe has become even more popular since Donnie Mac's has closed, and you are no longer able to purchase this delicious sandwich.

2 boneless skinless chicken breasts, halved and pounded to ¼-inch thickness

3 cups buttermilk, or enough to cover the chicken in a bowl

oil for frying

2 cups chopped cabbage

4 ciabatta buns

Breading

8 ounces panko bread crumbs

⅔ cup flour

1 teaspoon salt

2 teaspoons cayenne pepper

2 tablespoons garlic powder

1 tablespoon paprika

½ tablespoon thyme

Corn Slaw Sauce

½ cup whole-kernel corn

1 cup buttermilk

½ cup ranch dressing

3 tablespoons chopped green onion

salt and pepper to taste

1. Place chicken breasts in medium-sized bowl. Pour buttermilk over chicken until it is pretty much swimming in buttermilk. Refrigerate overnight.

2. To make the corn slaw sauce, sauté corn in a frying pan until it's a little caramelized, about 2–3 minutes. Coarsely chop corn in a food processor. Add buttermilk and ranch and pulse 1–2 times, until well mixed. Stir in green onion and add salt and pepper to taste. Set aside.

3. To make the breading, combine all breading ingredients in a shallow dish.

4. When you're ready to cook the chicken, place the chicken in bread crumbs. Press it down and let it sit on each side for a few seconds so the bread crumbs really stick on there.

5. Heat oil in a deep frying pan or deep fryer. Add breaded chicken. Fry until golden brown and cooked through.

6. Combine cabbage and ¼–½ cup of the sauce to make the slaw. You want the cabbage just covered in the sauce, not drowning in it. Do this right before putting it on the sandwich so it doesn't get soggy.

7. To serve, toast ciabatta in toaster or oven until slightly toasted. Add a little of the remaining corn slaw sauce to the bottom bun. Place fried chicken on bun, slap on some slaw, and top with remaining bun.

NOTE

For best results, marinate chicken breasts in buttermilk in the refrigerator for at least a couple of hours, or preferably overnight.

TURKEY SANDWICH WITH BRIE CHEESE AND APPLES

Inspired by **The Bluebird**, *Boise, Idaho*

TOTAL TIME: 5 MIN · SERVES 1

This sandwich is chock-full of creamy Brie cheese, tender turkey, and thinly sliced tart apple. The unique flavors blend together for one mouthwatering sandwich!

6 inches bakery artisan sandwich bread

3 tablespoons fig butter or fig preserves

¼ pound sliced or shaved deli turkey

2–3 ounces Brie cheese

½ cup spring mix

1 Granny Smith apple, thinly sliced

2 tablespoons Dijon mustard

1. Slice the bread in half. On the bottom half of the bread, generously spread the fig butter (as if you were making a PB&J).

2. Layer on the turkey, Brie (this can get tricky, just spread it on as best you can), greens, and apple.

3. Spread mustard on the top slice of bread and place on top of the sandwich. That's it! Seriously, best sandwich ever.

NOTES

• Get a good bread. We use French bread, which is wonderful, but you can use ciabatta, focaccia, or any kind of bread that looks delicious to you.

• This recipe calls for fig butter, and you can find it at Trader Joe's for just a couple of dollars. Fig butter really brings life to the sandwich; don't leave it out! If you don't have a Trader Joe's in your area, you can make your own by mixing fig preserves with softened butter, or you can just spread a layer of fig preserves on the bread. So yummy!

• Brie cheese is easy to find at your local grocery store. It can get a little sticky when spreading on the sandwich; you can just use your fingers to get an even layer.

• The tartness of the Granny Smith apple complements the creaminess of the cheese and just makes this sandwich so good. You won't use the entire apple—you just want a single layer—so slice up and serve the remaining apple on the side.

THANKSGIVING LEFTOVER, OR PILGRIM SANDWICH

Inspired by Capriotti's Sandwich Stop

TOTAL TIME: 10 MIN · MAKES 1 SANDWICH

This pilgrim sandwich is a delicious way to use up Thanksgiving leftovers. You take all the best parts of the big meal and pile them onto a sweet and savory sandwich. Our copycat is modeled after The Bobbie sandwich at Capriotti's.

1 Italian roll or 2 slices white bread

1 tablespoon cream cheese, softened

2 tablespoons cranberry sauce

2 slices turkey leftovers or deli turkey

¼ cup stuffing

1 slice provolone cheese

1 leaf romaine lettuce

1 tablespoon mayonnaise

1. Spread cream cheese on the bottom slice of bread. Add cranberry on top of the cream cheese.

2. Top with turkey, stuffing, provolone, and lettuce.

3. Spread some mayonnaise on the top half of the bread, then sandwich it together!

NOTE

Ideally you want to serve the sandwiches as soon as they are made. But, if you have leftovers, wrap the sandwich with plastic wrap and keep in the fridge. Serve within a day.

CHICKEN PESTO SANDWICH

Inspired by Cubby's

PREP TIME: 10 MIN · COOK TIME: 10 MIN · TOTAL TIME: 20 MIN · SERVES 2

This chicken pesto sandwich is our favorite at Cubby's. It has all of our favorite ingredients—bacon, pesto, cheese. You just can't go wrong!

1 boneless skinless chicken breast

olive oil, for drizzling

salt and pepper to taste

2 ciabatta rolls

2 tablespoons pesto

½ tablespoon mayonnaise

4 slices fresh mozzarella cheese

4 slices bacon, cooked

arugula

4 slices tomato

1. Cut chicken breast in half and pound it to thin it out. Drizzle olive oil over both sides and sprinkle with salt and pepper. Grill until cooked through.

2. While chicken is grilling, cut ciabatta rolls in half. Set aside.

3. Mix pesto and mayonnaise together and spread evenly over the ciabatta roll halves. Top with fresh mozzarella. On the top rack of the oven, broil on high until bread is golden brown on the edges and the cheese is slightly melted, about 2–3 minutes.

4. Add chicken, bacon, arugula, and tomatoes to each sandwich. Serve immediately.

NOTES

• If you're making this sandwich during the summer, go ahead and fire up the grill to cook the chicken. You can also use a grill pan on the stove or an indoor electric grill like a George Foreman, or you can bake it in the oven.

• Use fresh mozzarella for this sandwich for optimal melting and flavor.

• Ciabatta bread tastes delicious, but this would also taste great on our rosemary Parmesan focaccia bread. Find the recipe on our website, favfamilyrecipes.com.

TURKEY OVER ITALY

Inspired by Deli George, *Boise, Idaho*

TOTAL TIME: 10 MIN · SERVES 8

They make this Turkey over Italy Sandwich at our favorite deli in Boise called Deli George. It has turkey, provolone, and pesto mayo on focaccia bread.

1 loaf focaccia bread, cut into 8 wedges (like a pie)

1 pound smoked deli turkey (Get some good stuff. We like to get ours sliced thin, fresh from the deli.)

8 slices provolone cheese

½ cup sliced pepperoncini

1½ cups shredded lettuce

red wine vinegar, to taste

oregano, to taste

Pesto Mayo

1 cup mayonnaise

½ cup pesto

1. Mix together the mayonnaise and pesto in a small bowl. Set aside.

2. Toss shredded lettuce with red wine vinegar and a pinch of oregano. Set aside.

3. Cut open the focaccia bread wedges and layer each slice with the pesto mayo.

4. Layer each sandwich with turkey, provolone cheese, sliced pepperoncini, and shredded lettuce.

NOTE

This sandwich is perfect as is, but if you are looking to add more or don't have some of these ingredients on hand, try some other toppings.

- tomatoes
- thinly sliced red onions
- banana peppers
- spinach
- Monterey Jack cheese
- cheddar cheese
- salt and pepper

BEEF AND CHEDDAR

Inspired by Arby's

PREP TIME: 15 MIN · COOK TIME: 10 MIN · TOTAL TIME: 25 MIN · SERVES 8

The cheddar roast beef sandwich is always my go-to when we zip through the Arby's drive-thru. There's nothing quite like the combination of slices of tender roast combined with homemade melted cheddar and the signature tangy red ranch sauce. Each bite delivers a perfect balance of rich beef with creamy cheese.

1 pound thinly sliced deli roast beef, rare

8 onion hamburger buns

1 cup Arby's Sauce (see recipe on page 111)

Cheddar Cheese Sauce

2 teaspoons butter

2 tablespoons flour

approximately ¾ cup milk

1–2 cups shredded cheddar cheese (shredded by hand, not packaged)

salt and pepper to taste

1. Spray a medium-sized skillet with cooking spray. Cook roast beef in pan on medium until heated through. If desired, add a dash of beef broth to keep the meat juicy.

2. Make the Arby's Sauce and spread over one side of each bun. Place beef on bun. Make the cheddar cheese sauce by melting butter in a small saucepan over medium heat. Whisk in the flour, stirring constantly, and cook for about 1 minute, forming a roux.

3. *Slowly* whisk in milk until it reaches your desired consistency.

4. Remove from heat and stir in cheese. Add salt and pepper to taste.

5. Top meat with cheese sauce and serve.

NOTES
• Feel free to include some additions to your sandwich:
  - Add red onion for a fresh kick.
  - Use lettuce leaves for crunch and freshness.
  - Throw on jalapeños (pickled or fresh) for spice.
  - Slices of ripe tomatoes can make this slider very interesting.
  - Fried onion rings will add crunch and flavor.
• Packaged shredded cheese is often tossed with cornstarch, which means it won't easily melt into the sauce. We recommend shredding the cheese by hand for best results.
• If the milk and cheese mixture becomes thick, add a small amount of milk and whisk until smooth.

SAUCES AND DRESSINGS

CILANTRO LIME DRESSING

Inspired by **Cafe Rio** *and* **Costa Vida**

PREP TIME: 15 MIN · CHILL TIME: 2 HOURS · TOTAL TIME: 2 HOURS 15 MIN · SERVES 12

Cilantro lime dressing is a fresh and zesty dressing for all kinds of salads. This version is the perfect Cafe Rio and Costa Vida copycat!

2 tomatillos, husked and diced

½ bunch fresh cilantro

2 cloves garlic

1 tablespoon diced jalapeño

4 tablespoons fresh lime juice (approximately 2 limes)

1 tablespoon sugar

1 cup balsamic vinaigrette salad dressing (see notes)

1. In a food processor or blender, combine all ingredients. Mix well.
2. Refrigerate for at least 2 hours or overnight.

NOTES

• Make sure you use balsamic vinaigrette *salad dressing*, not balsamic vinegar.

• If you want less heat, remove the seeds from the jalapeño before dicing.

• Store leftovers in a mason jar with a lid and shake well before serving.

CREAMY TOMATILLO DRESSING

Inspired by **Cafe Rio**

PREP TIME: 10 MIN · CHILL TIME: 1 HOUR · TOTAL TIME: 1 HOUR 10 MIN · SERVES 16

This creamy tomatillo ranch dressing is so incredibly good. Try it over Cafe Rio-style salads, burritos, quesadillas, and more!

1 (1-ounce) packet Hidden Valley Ranch Seasoning (original, not buttermilk)

1 cup Best Foods mayonnaise

1 cup buttermilk

2 tomatillos, husked and diced

½ bunch fresh cilantro

1 clove garlic, peeled

1 teaspoon fresh lime juice

1 jalapeño, stem removed

1. Add all the ingredients to a blender. Blend until smooth. Chill for 1 hour.
2. Serve as a dressing over salad or as a dip for veggies and chips.

NOTE

If you like a thicker dressing, use only ½ cup buttermilk. If you like your dressing mild, remove the seeds from the jalapeño. We like it *spicy*, so we keep the seeds in it.

COPYCAT ARBY'S SAUCE

Inspired by **Arby's**

TOTAL TIME: 5 MIN · MAKES 6 SERVINGS

Re-create the iconic Arby's sauce flavor with a blend of tangy spices and a touch of sweetness. This recipe brings the unmistakable flavor of Arby's to your own kitchen.

½ cup ketchup

1 tablespoon apple cider vinegar

1 tablespoon brown sugar

2 tablespoons water

pinch of salt

¼ teaspoon garlic powder

½ teaspoon onion powder

Frank's RedHot Sauce, to taste (optional)

In a small saucepan combine all the sauce ingredients. Simmer over medium heat for a couple minutes, until warm and combined.

CAMPFIRE SAUCE

Inspired by **Red Robin**

TOTAL TIME: 5 MIN · MAKES 1¾ CUP

This Red Robin Campfire Sauce tastes exactly like the smoky sauce at the popular restaurant. Make it at home and enjoy that tangy taste on your burgers, fries, and more. And it takes only two ingredients!

1 cup mayonnaise

¾ cup barbecue sauce

thick cut French fries or steak fries, for dipping

1. Combine mayonnaise and barbecue sauce in a bowl. Stir until well combined.

2. Serve with fries.

NOTE

For the mayonnaise, we like Best Foods or Hellmann's brand. For the barbecue sauce, we like to use Bull's Eye Original Barbecue Sauce. For a more smoky flavor, use Sweet Baby Ray's Hickory and Brown Sugar Barbecue Sauce.

HOMEMADE CHICK-FIL-A SAUCE

Inspired by Chick-fil-A

TOTAL TIME: 3 MIN · MAKES ABOUT 1½ CUPS

Our copycat sauce tastes like the real deal. It's so easy and takes only four ingredients!

1 cup Best Foods mayonnaise

¼ cup yellow or Dijon mustard

¼ cup honey

3 tablespoons ketchup or barbecue sauce

1. Combine all ingredients in a small mixing bowl. Stir or whisk together until well combined.
2. Serve with chicken nuggets, waffle fries, or any of the suggestions in the notes.

NOTE

Serve this sauce with any of the following:

- Chicken: Chicken nuggets, grilled chicken, or chicken sandwiches always go well with this sauce.
- Fries: This sauce tastes especially yummy on sweet potato fries!
- Burgers: Spread this on hamburgers instead of ketchup and mayo.
- Sandwiches and Wraps: This sauce pairs perfectly with turkey, ham, or roast beef sandwiches.
- Salads: Drizzle some sauce over your crispy chicken salad.
- Veggies: Dip broccoli, carrots, celery, pea pods, or cauliflower in this sauce.
- Tacos: Dress up your Taco Tuesday with a healthy dollop of this sauce!

BLUE CHEESE DRESSING

Inspired by Outback Steakhouse

PREP TIME: 5 MIN · CHILL TIME: 3 HOURS · TOTAL TIME: 3 HOURS 5 MIN · SERVES 12

When it comes to salad dressings, blue cheese is always a favorite. With this simple recipe, you can keep it in the fridge for up to a week and have it on hand anytime to use as a salad dressing, as a dip for buffalo wings and fresh veggies, or on sandwiches and wraps.

1 cup Best Foods mayonnaise

1 cup sour cream

¼ cup buttermilk

¼ cup blue cheese crumbles, plus ½ cup for topping

1 teaspoon distilled white vinegar

1 teaspoon Worcestershire sauce

½ teaspoon minced garlic

½ teaspoon lemon juice

⅛ teaspoon salt

⅛ teaspoon pepper

1. In a blender, combine all ingredients except for the reserved ½ cup blue cheese crumbles. Blend until thoroughly mixed and smooth.

2. Pour dressing into bowl and gently stir in remaining crumbles. Refrigerate 3 hours or overnight before serving.

SIDE DISHES

BREADTWISTS

Inspired by Pizza Factory

PREP TIME: 10 MIN · RISE TIME: 35 MIN · COOK TIME: 20 MIN
TOTAL TIME: 1 HOUR 5 MIN · SERVES 6

These breadsticks are so easy to make and complement any meal from soup to spaghetti. They're fluffy, buttery, and oh so yummy!

Dough

1½ cups warm water

2 tablespoons sugar

1 tablespoon active dry yeast

3½ cups flour

1 teaspoon salt

Topping

½ cup butter, melted and divided

2 teaspoons minced garlic, divided

½ teaspoon kosher salt

1 teaspoon dried basil

1 teaspoon dried oregano

¼ cup grated Parmesan cheese

Marinara Sauce

2 tablespoons olive oil

1 tablespoon minced garlic

1 (6-ounce) can tomato paste

1 (8-ounce) can tomato sauce

2 teaspoons basil

2 teaspoons oregano

2 teaspoons salt, or to taste

Breadsticks

1. In a large mixing bowl or the bowl of a stand mixer fitted with a dough hook, mix water, sugar, and yeast. Let sit for 5 minutes. Add flour and salt. Mix until smooth. Cover and let rise for 10 minutes.

2. On a floured surface, roll the dough out into a square. The dough should be about a ¼-inch thick. Mix ¼ cup butter and 1 teaspoon minced garlic together. Spread the garlic butter over the whole dough square. Sprinkle with salt.

3. Fold the square in half and cut the dough into 1-inch-wide strips with a pizza cutter. Twist each strip and place on a baking sheet. Let rise for 20 minutes.

4. Bake at 400 degrees F. for 20 minutes or until golden brown.

5. While the breadsticks are still warm, melt the remaining butter and add 1 teaspoon minced garlic, kosher salt, basil, and oregano. Brush the herb butter over the breadsticks and top with Parmesan cheese.

6. Serve with marinara, ranch, or Alfredo sauce for dipping.

Marinara Sauce

1. For homemade marinara, heat olive oil in a skillet over medium heat. Sauté garlic in olive oil. Add tomato paste, tomato sauce, basil, oregano, and salt. Simmer on low for 15 minutes.

COLESLAW

Inspired by KFC

TOTAL TIME: 15 MIN · SERVES 16

This crunchy coleslaw tastes just like what KFC serves at its restaurants, but for a fraction of the price! It's the perfect side dish for barbecues and potlucks.

8 cups finely chopped cabbage

¼ cup julienned carrots

⅓ cup sugar

⅛ teaspoon salt

⅛ teaspoon pepper

½ cup milk

½ cup mayonnaise

½ cup buttermilk

1½ tablespoons distilled white vinegar

2½ tablespoons lemon juice

1½ teaspoons yellow mustard (optional)

1. In a large bowl, toss cabbage with carrots. Set aside.

2. In a separate bowl, combine all remaining ingredients. Whisk until smooth. Pour over cabbage and carrots. Mix well.

3. Cover and refrigerate until ready to serve.

NOTES

• To save time, you can use a packaged bag of shredded cabbage instead of chopping your own.

• The mustard is optional, but we think it adds a nice flavor.

• It's okay to serve this dish immediately, but it's best if you let it sit overnight. It can even keep for up to 2–3 days, but you should discard it once it starts to get mushy.

CHOW MEIN

Inspired by **Panda Express**

PREP TIME: 20 MIN · COOK TIME: 5 MIN · TOTAL TIME: 25 MIN · SERVES 8

Our chow mein copycat recipe is easy to make and tastes just like the Panda Express side dish. Make a healthier version of this chow mein at home for a fraction of the price!

¼ cup soy sauce

1 tablespoon brown sugar

2 cloves garlic, minced

1 teaspoon grated fresh ginger

ground black pepper, to taste

3 (5.6-ounce) packages refrigerated Yakisoba noodles

⅔ cup diagonally chopped celery

1 medium onion, thinly sliced

2 cups chopped cabbage

1. In a small bowl, combine soy sauce, brown sugar, garlic, ginger, and black pepper. Set aside.

2. Remove noodles from packages and discard included flavoring packets. Rinse noodles well, drain, and set aside.

3. Heat oil in a large wok or skillet over medium heat. Add celery and onion and sauté for 1–2 minutes or until onions start to become soft and transparent. Add cabbage and sauté an additional minute.

4. Add noodles and soy sauce mixture to the vegetables. Stir-fry over medium-high heat for an additional 2–3 minutes or until noodles are heated through.

NOTES

• In this recipe, you can add a shake or two of sesame oil to the vegetable oil to add a deeper flavor, but don't overdo it! We aren't including it in the recipe because the sesame oil flavoring can become overpowering really quickly if you aren't careful. We have made it both ways (with and without sesame oil), and they both taste great.

• Feel free to add more vegetables or a variety of vegetables to your chow mein. Just because Panda Express uses only onions and celery doesn't mean you have to limit yourself!

• Yakisoba noodles can be found in the produce section of the grocery store. Usually the three packages are sold together in a single 17-ounce pack.

• Don't overcook the noodles. Overcooking them can cause them to break. You want them to be just heated through.

ELOTE IN A CUP, OR MEXICAN STREET CORN CUPS

Inspired by Cozy Cone, *Cars Land, Disney California Adventure Park*

PREP TIME: 10 MIN · COOK TIME: 5 MIN · TOTAL TIME: 15 MIN · SERVES 4

This elote in a cup is an explosion of all the classic Mexican street corn flavors but served in a cup for easier eating.

Elote

1 cup water

2 tablespoons sugar

1 pound frozen whole-kernel corn

¼ cup mayonnaise

¼ cup sour cream

½ teaspoon sriracha sauce, or to taste

kosher salt, to taste

lime salt, to taste (optional)

Toppings

½ cup crumbled cotija cheese or queso fresco

¼ cup cilantro

dash of chili powder

4 lime wedges

1. In a medium saucepan over high, bring water and sugar to a boil. When water is boiling, add corn and cover with lid. Simmer corn for 3–5 minutes or until corn is cooked through and tender.

2. While corn is simmering, combine mayonnaise, sour cream, sriracha, salt, and lime salt in a small bowl.

3. When corn is done cooking, drain well and return to pan. Allow to cool for about 3 minutes. Add sriracha-mayo mixture to the corn and stir until well combined.

4. Divide corn into 4 individual cups. Top with cheese or queso fresco, cilantro, a dash of chili powder, and a lime wedge. Serve immediately.

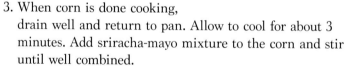

MEXICAN-STYLE BLACK BEANS

Inspired by Cafe Rio

PREP TIME: 5 MIN · COOK TIME: 10 MIN · TOTAL TIME: 15 MIN · SERVES 4

Black beans are a great addition to any Mexican-inspired meal! Serve them with rice as a side dish or inside of your favorite burritos and tacos.

2 tablespoons olive oil

2 cloves garlic, minced

1 teaspoon cumin

1 (15-ounce) can black beans, undrained

1⅓ cups tomato juice

½ teaspoon salt

2 tablespoons chopped cilantro

1. Heat oil over medium heat in a large pan. Add garlic and cumin and cook for a few minutes, until the garlic is fragrant.

2. Add beans, tomato juice, and salt. Cook until heated through, stirring frequently.

3. Just before serving, stir in the cilantro.

NOTES

• If the beans are looking too dry, add a little water or chicken broth to the mixture.

• Be sure to use tomato juice, not tomato sauce, in this recipe.

CILANTRO LIME RICE

Inspired by **Chipotle**

PREP TIME: 10 MIN · COOK TIME: 20 MIN · TOTAL TIME: 30 MIN · SERVES 4

With these simple steps and key ingredients like fluffy rice, fresh cilantro, and zingy lime, you can bring the distinctive flavors of Chipotle to your dinner table. This rice pairs well with any Mexican dish.

1 cup basmati rice

1 teaspoon olive oil

½ teaspoon minced garlic

2 cups chicken broth

1 tablespoon butter

¼ cup lime juice

¾ cup fresh cilantro, finely chopped

1. Rinse rice and place in a medium pot or saucepan. Add olive oil and garlic and sauté over medium heat for 2 minutes.

2. Slowly add chicken broth and bring to a boil. Reduce heat to medium-low and simmer, uncovered, until water level drops below the surface of the rice, about 4 minutes.

3. Reduce heat to low and cover pan with lid. Do not stir. Cook for 11 minutes. Remove from heat and let sit with lid on for 5 minutes.

4. Remove the lid and add butter, lime juice, and cilantro. Let sit for about 2 more minutes. Fluff rice with fork or rice paddle and serve.

HOMEMADE ANIMAL STYLE FRIES

Inspired by In-N-Out

PREP TIME: 10 MIN · COOK TIME: 20 MIN · TOTAL TIME: 30 MIN · SERVES 6

These loaded fries taste *just* like the "secret menu" favorite. In less time than it takes to go to In-N-Out, you can enjoy these popular smothered fries at home!

Fries

1 (2-pound) bag frozen French fries

1 tablespoon butter or vegetable oil

1 cup finely chopped white or yellow onion

pinch of sea salt

6 slices American cheese (Kraft or Velveeta brand)

Homemade In-N-Out Sauce

⅔ cup mayonnaise

⅓ cup ketchup

2 tablespoons sweet relish

1 tablespoon yellow mustard

1. Prepare fries according to package directions. I like them best when made in an air fryer. If baking, you can bake them on a baking sheet lined with parchment paper to be ready for broiling them with cheese later.

2. While fries are baking, sauté onions. Melt butter in a nonstick skillet over medium-high heat. Add the diced onions to the pan and sprinkle with salt. Sauté until the onions become golden brown with crisp edges. Remove from heat and set aside.

3. Prepare the sauce by combining all the sauce ingredients in a small bowl. Set aside until ready to add to the fries.

4. When fries are heated, place them on a baking sheet lined with parchment paper if you haven't already. Put the fries close together and place the slices of cheese over the top so they cover most of the surface of the fries. Turn the oven to broil. Place pan under the broiler for 1–2 minutes or until cheese has melted.

5. Remove the cheese-covered fries from the oven. You can leave them on the baking tray or place them on a serving platter. Add a few scoops of the prepared sauce over the top. Spoon the cooked onion over the top of the sauce and serve.

HAWAIIAN MACARONI SALAD

Inspired by **L&L Barbecue**

PREP TIME: 20 MIN · COOK TIME: 15 MIN · CHILL TIME: 4 HOURS 15 MIN
TOTAL TIME: 4 HOURS 50 MIN · SERVES 10

This Hawaiian macaroni salad is the real deal. It's a no-frills, creamy mac salad that is the perfect side dish for any barbecue or luau!

1 pound macaroni

2 tablespoons apple cider vinegar

2 carrots, shredded

¼ cup shredded onion (optional)

2½ cups mayonnaise

¼ cup milk

2 teaspoons sugar

kosher salt, to taste

ground black pepper, to taste

1. Cook macaroni according to package directions. Drain well and place in a large bowl.

2. While macaroni is still hot, sprinkle on vinegar. Add carrots and onion. Toss together until well combined. Refrigerate for 15 minutes, or until cooled.

3. In a separate small bowl, whisk together mayo, milk, and sugar. Fold mayo mixture into the macaroni until all the noodles are evenly coated. Add salt and pepper to taste.

4. Cover and refrigerate at least 4 hours (best if overnight).

5. Gently stir before serving. Add a little more milk if needed, no more than a tablespoon or two.

NOTES

• Put boiled macaroni and ingredients directly in a Tupperware bowl with a lid for easy refrigeration.

• Make sure you use Best Foods or Hellmann's mayonnaise—no substitutes!

CREAMED SPINACH

Inspired by **Ruth's Chris Steak House**

PREP TIME: 5 MIN · COOK TIME: 10 MIN · TOTAL TIME: 15 MIN · SERVES 8

This is the best creamed spinach recipe you'll ever taste! Three kinds of cheese and vibrant spinach, together with fragrant herbs, make this a favorite dish at Thanksgiving—or anytime.

20–24 ounces (about 1½ pounds) fresh spinach

5 tablespoons butter

1 onion, finely chopped

4 cloves garlic, crushed

¼ cup flour

2 cups half-and-half

kosher salt, to taste

ground black pepper, to taste

½ cup fresh shredded Parmesan cheese (not the powdered kind)

½ cup mozzarella cheese

5 wedges Laughing Cow Creamy Swiss Original cheese or 4 ounces cream cheese

1. Bring a large stockpot of water to a boil. Add spinach and cook for 2–3 minutes or until spinach is wilted but not soggy. Drain spinach well and then wring it out using cheesecloth (preferred) or a kitchen towel. You can also press spinach in a fine mesh strainer to remove excess water. Set spinach aside.

2. In a large skillet over medium heat, melt butter. Add onions and garlic and cook until onions become soft and transparent.

3. Sprinkle flour over the onions and stir until flour is cooked, about 3 minutes. Pour in half-and-half a little at a time, whisking constantly, to make a béchamel sauce. You want it to be the consistency of a thin gravy. Add more half-and-half or milk if needed. Add salt and pepper to taste.

4. Add spinach and stir until spinach is well mixed in.

5. Add Parmesan, mozzarella, and Creamy Swiss cheese. Stir until all cheeses are melted and completely mixed in. Serve immediately.

NOTES

• Unsalted butter is best so you can control the amount of sodium in the recipe.

• You can substitute whole milk and a splash of heavy cream if you don't have half-and-half on hand.

• Fresh baby spinach is best, but you can substitute a package of frozen spinach. The trick is to thaw it completely and press out as much water as possible. After it's been cooked, the spinach may be *very* hot. Handle it with care and allow it to cool if needed. You may be surprised to find that you have only 1-2 cups of spinach after you've cooked it and pressed the water out. This is totally normal.

MAIN DISHES

MIZITHRA PASTA

Inspired by **The Old Spaghetti Factory**

PREP TIME: 5 MIN · COOK TIME: 9 MIN · TOTAL TIME: 14 MIN · SERVES 4–6

Our version of The Old Spaghetti Factory's mizithra pasta is *amazing*. It is a rich and buttery dish that your whole family will love.

1 cup butter (no substitutes)

16 ounces spaghetti noodles, cooked and drained

6 ounces mizithra cheese, finely grated, divided

fresh basil, for garnish (optional)

1. Slowly melt butter in a small saucepan over medium heat until golden brown, about 5 minutes. The butter will foam up and rise, but just keep stirring until it turns brown.

2. Remove pan from heat and pour melted butter into a tempered glass bowl or measuring bowl. Allow the sediment to settle at the bottom of the bowl for a few minutes. Do not stir up the sediment; you want the clear butter separated from the sediment at the bottom.

3. Pour the browned butter into a separate bowl, keeping the butter separated from the sediment. Discard the sediment.

4. Toss the cooked pasta with the butter. Reserve ½ cup mizithra cheese. Stir the remaining cheese into the butter-coated pasta. Sprinkle reserved ½ cup cheese on top. Garnish with sliced fresh basil. Serve immediately.

NOTE

The most important thing to remember when making brown butter is to boil it over medium heat. You don't want it to burn! Use a pan with a light-colored bottom (like white, rather than black) so you can see the color of the butter easier at the bottom of the pan. Once the butter melts and gets hot, it will start to foam. If you pick up the pan and swirl it around a little it can help you see the color through the foam. Once the butter turns a deep golden brown and you start to smell a little bit of a nutty smell, it is ready! Transfer it to a heat-safe small bowl and let the milk particles sink to the bottom while it cools. Then transfer it to a different bowl, trying to leave most of the solid particles behind. You can also strain it through a cheesecloth or fine mesh strainer.

ORANGE CHICKEN

Inspired by **Panda Express**

PREP TIME: 20 MIN · COOK TIME: 20 MIN · TOTAL TIME: 40 MIN · SERVES 6

This orange chicken recipe tastes just like the popular Panda Express dish, but it's made with simple ingredients right at home. Tender chicken in tangy sauce beats restaurant takeout any day.

Chicken

2 pounds boneless skinless chicken thighs or breasts

1 cup cornstarch

½ teaspoon salt

¼ teaspoon pepper

1 egg, beaten

vegetable oil, for frying

Orange Sauce

3 tablespoons cornstarch

1¼ cup water, divided

2 tablespoons fresh orange juice

¼ cup fresh lemon juice

⅓ cup rice vinegar

3 tablespoons soy sauce

1 cup brown sugar

1 tablespoon orange zest

1 teaspoon minced fresh ginger root

1 teaspoon minced garlic

2 tablespoons chopped green onion, plus more for garnish

red pepper flakes, to taste

Chicken

1. Cut chicken into bite-size pieces. Combine cornstarch, salt, and pepper in a resealable plastic bag. Dip chicken in beaten egg. Shake chicken in cornstarch mixture to coat.

2. Heat oil in a deep fryer or wok to 375 degrees F. Deep-fry chicken in batches until completely cooked. Remove to drain on paper towels.

Orange Sauce

1. In a small bowl, combine cornstarch with ¼ cup water and mix thoroughly. Set aside.

2. In a large saucepan combine remaining 1 cup water, orange juice, lemon juice, rice vinegar, and soy sauce. Whisk ingredients together over medium heat for a few minutes.

3. Stir in brown sugar, orange zest, ginger, garlic, and green onion. Bring to a boil. Slowly stir cornstarch mixture into sauce until it thickens.

4. Place fried chicken in a large bowl and pour sauce over the top. Fold the sauce into the chicken or toss gently to coat. If desired, add red pepper flakes and garnish with green onion.

CHICAGO-STYLE DEEP-DISH PIZZA

Inspired by Gino's East Pizzeria

PREP TIME: 30 MIN · REST TIME: OVERNIGHT · COOK TIME: 45 MIN
TOTAL TIME: 1 HOUR 15 MIN PLUS OVERNIGHT · SERVES 8

This Chicago-style deep-dish pizza is so incredibly good. It's a meaty, cheesy pizza with a delicious homemade sauce.

Crust

1 cup lukewarm water

1 (.25-ounce) packet active dry yeast

1 tablespoon sugar

⅓ cup corn oil

1 teaspoon cream of tartar

1 pound bread flour

Pizza Sauce

1 (28-ounce) can San Marzano tomatoes, undrained

½ teaspoon salt

½ teaspoon dried basil

½ teaspoon dried oregano

¼ teaspoon fresh ground black pepper

Toppings

16 ounces shredded mozzarella

25 slices pepperoni

10 ounces Italian sausage, uncooked, pinched into little pieces

Crust

1. In a bowl, combine water, yeast, sugar, oil, and cream of tartar. Mix with your hand or a whisk until yeast dissolves.

2. Pour in bread flour a little at a time. Mix with your hand or a dough mixer. Knead until firm, about 10 minutes. Add more flour if needed.

3. Brush a bowl with oil. Roll dough into a ball and put it in the bowl. Cover with plastic wrap and a kitchen towel. Let sit on the counter overnight.

Pizza Sauce

1. Pour tomatoes into a bowl. Using a potato masher or just your hands, mash the tomatoes up so that there are no chunks bigger than a quarter.

2. Add the rest of the sauce ingredients and stir. Adjust the salt and pepper to taste. Do not use too much basil or oregano.

Assembly

1. Heat oven to 350 degrees F.

2. Prepare a 14-inch deep-dish pizza pan or a round cake pan with straight sides by coating the inside of it with a very healthy coating of melted butter or oil.

3. Roll the dough out to about 3 inches larger in diameter than the bottom of the pan, then place inside the pan and pinch the dough up along the sides.

4. Sprinkle the cheese on the crust, add the pepperoni and sausage pieces, and cover with the sauce.

5. Bake about 45 minutes, until the crust starts to brown and cheese starts to bubble up through the sauce. The little edges of the pepperoni should also start to crisp, and the sausage should be cooked through.

NOTES

- Don't like the toppings? Swap them out for your favorites!

- Try to get tomatoes with the DOP label so you know they are real Italian tomatoes.

- Use low-moisture part-skim mozzarella, not low-fat. It won't turn out well if you use low-fat.

- To prep ahead, make the sauce in advance. It will stay good in the fridge for up to a week.

- To store, keep leftovers in an airtight container in the fridge for up to 1 week, or in the freezer for up to 1 month.

SWEET PORK BURRITOS

Inspired by Cafe Rio

PREP TIME: 30 MIN · MARINATE TIME: 4 HOURS · COOK TIME: 10 HOURS 30 MIN
TOTAL TIME: 15 HOURS · SERVES 10

Smothered in enchilada sauce, this sweet pork burrito copycat recipe tastes just like the original.

Sweet Pork

2 pounds pork (boneless pork ribs work best)

3 (12-ounce) cans Coca-Cola (not diet)

¼ cup brown sugar

Dash garlic salt

¼ cup water

1 can diced green chilies

1 (10-ounce) can red enchilada sauce

1 cup brown sugar

Sauce

1 (4-ounce) can diced green chiles

7 ounces salsa verde

½ cup chicken broth

2 teaspoons sugar

1 teaspoon salt

Burrito

1 large flour tortilla

½ cup cilantro lime rice

½ cup black beans

¾ cup sweet pork

½ cup shredded Monterey Jack cheese, divided

lettuce, for serving

pico de gallo, for serving

guacamole, for serving

Sweet Pork

1. Put the pork in a heavy-duty zip-top plastic bag to marinate. Add about a can and a half of Coke and ¼ cup of brown sugar. Marinate in the fridge for 4 hours or overnight.

2. Drain marinade and put pork, ½ can of Coke, water, and garlic salt in a slow-cooker on high for about 3–4 hours or on low for 8 hours. (You want the meat to shred easily, but not be too dry.)

3. Remove pork from slow cooker and discard any liquid left in the pot. Shred pork.

4. In a food processor or blender, blend ½ can Coke, chilies, enchilada sauce, and 1 cup brown sugar. If the mixture looks too thick, add more Coke little by little. Put shredded pork and sauce in slow cooker and cook on low for 2 hours.

Sauce

1. Combine all the sauce ingredients in a small saucepan. Bring to a boil, then reduce heat to low and simmer for at least 20 minutes.

Assembly

1. Heat oven to 450 degrees F.

2. Layer rice, beans, pork, and ¼ cup cheese on top of the tortilla. Roll it up into a burrito. Pour about ½ cup green enchilada sauce over the burrito and top with remaining ¼ cup cheese. Bake until cheese is melted, about 5–7 minutes.

3. Serve with lettuce, pico de gallo, and guacamole.

NOTES

• Visit favfamilyrecipes.com for our recipes for homemade tortillas, cilantro lime rice, black beans, sweet pork, and guacamole.

HAWAIIAN PORK

Inspired by Mo'Bettahs

PREP TIME: 10 MIN · COOK TIME: 8 HOURS · TOTAL TIME: 8 HOURS 10 MIN · SERVES 16

Kalua pork is a Hawaiian dish often served at luaus. This version is made in the slow cooker and tastes just like authentic shredded kalua pig.

1 (3-to-4-pound) pork roast

1–2 tablespoons kosher salt

⅓ cup liquid smoke

1 cup water

½ head cabbage, coarsely chopped (optional)

1. Rub pork generously with salt. Place the pork in a slow cooker. Pour on liquid smoke. Add water. Cover and cook on low for 8–10 hours.

2. An hour before serving, carefully lift pork out of the slow cooker. Do not drain out juices. Place cabbage in the bottom of the slow cooker. Place pork on top of the cabbage, place lid back on, and cook for another hour. Shred pork and serve.

HAWAIIAN CHICKEN RICE BOWLS

Inspired by Rumbi Island Grill

PREP TIME: 10 MIN · COOK TIME: 20 MIN · TOTAL TIME: 30 MIN · SERVES 6

This easy teriyaki chicken rice bowl recipe makes a delicious, fast, and nutritious meal. It's one of our favorite entrees at Rumbi—the flavor is so good!

2 cups cubed grilled chicken

Hawaiian Coconut Rice and Beans

2½ cups water

½ tablespoon sugar

1 (14-ounce) can coconut milk

1 (14-ounce can) red beans, drained and rinsed

2 cups long-grain white rice

Hawaiian Teriyaki Sauce

¾ cup Mr. Yoshida's Original Gourmet Sweet Teriyaki Marinade & Cooking Sauce

2 teaspoons chili garlic sauce

1 teaspoon soy sauce

1 teaspoon grated fresh ginger

¼ teaspoon salt

¼ teaspoon brown sugar

1 tablespoon cornstarch

2 tablespoons cold water

1–2 teaspoons sriracha sauce (optional)

Stir-Fry Vegetables

1 tablespoon vegetable oil

4 carrots, peeled and grated

3 ribs celery, sliced

1 zucchini, cubed

1½ cups chopped broccoli florets

Hawaiian Coconut Rice and Beans

1. Rice Cooker: Combine all ingredients in a rice cooker. Gently stir so the beans and rice are mixed. Cover and cook. Fluff rice with a fork before serving.

2. Stovetop: In a saucepan, combine water, sugar, and coconut milk. Stir in beans and rice. Bring to a boil over medium heat. Cover, reduce heat, and simmer 18–20 minutes, until rice is tender.

Hawaiian Teriyaki Sauce

1. Combine Yoshida's sauce, chili garlic sauce, soy sauce, ginger, salt, and brown sugar in a small saucepan. Bring to a boil, then reduce heat to a simmer.

2. Mix cornstarch and water together in a small bowl. Slowly whisk the cornstarch mixture into the simmering sauce. This will thicken the sauce slightly more.

3. For a spicier sauce, add 1–2 shakes of sriracha sauce. Simmer for about 1 minute, then let sit until ready to serve.

Stir-Fry Vegetables

1. Heat vegetable oil in a large skillet over medium-high heat. Sauté carrots, celery, zucchini, and broccoli until crisp-tender, about 2 minutes.

Assembly

1. To serve, scoop rice and beans into the bottom of each bowl. Add vegetables and chicken. Serve teriyaki sauce on the side, or evenly drizzle about 3 tablespoons over vegetables.

NOTE

Don't have time to grill? You can also use packaged grilled chicken, found in most grocery stores. Cut the chicken into cubes and sauté in a skillet with a little oil until heated.

MEDITERRANEAN BOWLS

Inspired by **The White House Grill**, *Post Falls, Idaho*

PREP TIME: 25 MIN · CHILL TIME: 1 HOUR · COOK TIME: 35 MIN
TOTAL TIME: 1 HOUR 35 MIN · SERVES 2

This Mediterranean bowl recipe is a fresh and delicious lunch or dinner option! Topped with chicken, feta, cucumbers, and all kinds of favorite Greek flavors, you'll get Mediterranean flair in every bite.

Lemon Pepper Chicken

2 boneless skinless chicken breasts

1 cup Lawry's Lemon Pepper Marinade

lemon pepper seasoning, to taste

Yellow Rice

1½ tablespoons butter

½ cup long grain rice

½ teaspoon minced garlic

½ teaspoon onion powder

½ teaspoon ground turmeric

1 cup chicken broth

¼ teaspoon kosher salt

1 tablespoon fresh cilantro

Toppings

2 cups fresh spinach

1 cup diced chicken

½ cup fire-roasted corn

½ cup diced cucumber

½ cup tzatziki sauce

crumbled feta

pickled red onions

fresh dill

toasted pita bread, for serving

Lemon Pepper Chicken

1. Combine chicken breasts and lemon pepper marinade in a resealable plastic bag. Chill for at least 1 hour.

2. Heat oven to 350 degrees F. Remove chicken from bag and discard marinade.

3. Place chicken in a 9x13-inch glass baking dish. Sprinkle with lemon pepper seasoning on both sides. Bake for 35 minutes, or until juices run clear and chicken is completely cooked through. Once cooled, dice for using in the bowl.

Yellow Rice

1. Heat butter in a saucepan over medium heat. Add the rice and gently stir until rice begins to lightly brown.

2. Add garlic, onion powder, and turmeric and mix well.

3. Slowly stir in chicken broth and raise heat to medium-high. Add salt and pepper to taste.

4. Bring the mix to a boil, then turn the heat to low and cover the pan with a lid. Simmer for 20 minutes.

6. Remove from heat. Add fresh cilantro and fluff with a fork.

Assembly

1. In a large bowl, combine rice and spinach. Top with chicken, corn, cucumber, tzatziki, feta, pickled red onions, and fresh dill. Serve with toasted pita bread.

NOTE

To make your own tzatziki sauce, combine 1 cup plain Greek yogurt, ½ cup cucumber (peeled, seeded, and diced), 1 teaspoon fresh dill, 1 teaspoon fresh lemon juice, salt and pepper (to taste) in a food processor or blender. Blend until well combined.

INDONESIAN PEANUT SATAY

Inspired by **Noodles and Company**

PREP TIME: 10 MIN · COOK TIME: 25 MIN · TOTAL TIME: 35 MIN · SERVES 8

When we learned that Noodles and Company was taking this dish off the menu, we knew we had to replicate it at home. We used the basic components—noodles, veggies, chicken, and peanut sauce—and set out to make our own version. Don't be intimidated by the long list of ingredients. They are pantry staples, and you can take out or add anything you like to this very versatile dish.

2 pounds chicken, cut into thin strips

vegetable oil

1 tablespoon sriracha sauce

1 lime, juiced

3 cloves garlic, pressed

1 tablespoon fresh ginger, minced

4 teaspoons soy sauce

salt and pepper to taste

16 ounces linguine noodles

1 cup shoestring carrots

2 cups broccoli florets, chopped

½ cup green onion, chopped

1 cup bean sprouts

peanuts, for garnish

2 lime slices, for garnish

Peanut Sauce

1 cup chicken broth

6 tablespoons creamy peanut butter, heaping

2–4 teaspoons sriracha sauce, or to taste

3 tablespoons honey

6 tablespoons soy sauce

3 tablespoons fresh ginger, minced

4–5 cloves garlic, pressed or minced

1. In a large skillet, add oil and sauté chicken, sriracha, lime juice, garlic, ginger, soy sauce, salt, and pepper.
2. While chicken is cooking, prepare the linguine (to al dente) and make the peanut sauce. After the chicken is cooked, remove from the skillet and wrap in foil to keep warm.
3. Re-oil the skillet, add all vegetables except bean sprouts and sauté.
4. Add the chicken and bean sprouts to the skillet, cover, reduce heat, and simmer for 2–3 minutes.
5. Drain noodles and combine with the peanut sauce.
6. Top with veggies and chicken.
7. Garnish with peanuts and limes.

Peanut Sauce

1. Combine chicken broth, peanut butter, sriracha, honey, soy sauce, ginger, and garlic in a small saucepan over medium-low heat until sauce becomes smooth and well blended.

NOTE

Try any of these additional ingredients:

- green bell peppers
- shredded coconut
- sesame seeds
- tamari
- snap peas
- scallions or shallots
- mushrooms, sliced into bite-size pieces
- dried red peppers

HOMEMADE MALIBU CHICKEN

Inspired by **Sizzler**

PREP TIME: 15 MIN · COOK TIME: 35 MIN · MARINATE TIME: 4 HOURS
TOTAL TIME: 4 HOURS 50 MIN · SERVES 4

This chicken copycat recipe tastes even better than the popular restaurant dish! You'll love the fresh, crispy chicken and tangy mustard sauce.

3 egg yolks

2 cloves garlic, minced

2 boneless skinless chicken breasts, halved

6 tablespoons butter

1 cup panko bread crumbs

1 cup grated Parmesan cheese

1 tablespoon dried parsley

1 tablespoon garlic powder

½ tablespoon salt

ground black pepper, to taste

4 slices Black Forest ham or deli ham

4 slices Swiss cheese

Honey Mustard Sauce

3 tablespoons mayonnaise

2 tablespoons Grey Poupon Dijon mustard

1 teaspoon yellow mustard

1 teaspoon honey

1. In a small bowl, beat egg yolks with garlic. Combine chicken and egg mixture in a large resealable plastic bag, squeeze out all the air, and seal tightly. Place chicken in the refrigerator and allow to marinate for 4 hours or overnight.

2. Heat oven to 400 degrees F. Melt butter and pour into bottom of a 9x13-inch baking dish. Set aside.

3. In a bowl, mix bread crumbs, Parmesan cheese, parsley, garlic powder, salt, and pepper.

4. Dip marinated chicken in crumb mixture. Place coated chicken in baking dish, and pour remaining egg mixture over the top.

5. Bake for 15 minutes on each side or until chicken is no longer pink and juices run clear.

6. Top each piece of chicken with ham and a slice of Swiss cheese. Place back in the oven for about 5 minutes or until cheese is melted.

7. Remove from oven and serve with honey mustard sauce.

Honey Mustard Sauce

1. Mix the honey mustard sauce ingredients together and refrigerate until ready to serve.

NOTES

• This chicken tastes so good the next day sliced up on a bun for a sandwich. Just add some lettuce and tomatoes and slice the chicken into strips.

• Store leftovers in an airtight container and refrigerate for up to 5 days. It is best to store the cooked chicken before adding the ham and cheese. If the cheese is added before storing, it will melt too quickly when reheating. Reheat chicken in an air fryer at 350 degrees F. for 8–9 minutes or until cooked through, add ham and cheese the last 2 minutes.

COPYCAT ALICE SPRINGS CHICKEN

Inspired by Outback Steakhouse

PREP TIME: 10 MIN · MARINATE TIME: 2 HOURS · COOK TIME: 20 MIN
TOTAL TIME: 2 HOURS 30 MIN · SERVES 8

This chicken is smothered in cheese, bacon, and mushrooms—so easy to make at home!

2 cups sliced white mushrooms

2 tablespoons butter

4 boneless skinless chicken breasts, halved

1 tablespoon vegetable oil

salt and pepper, to taste

paprika, to taste

8 slices bacon, cooked

1 cup shredded Monterey Jack cheese

1 cup shredded cheddar cheese

2 teaspoons fresh parsley, finely chopped

Honey Mustard Marinade

1 cup Grey Poupon Dijon mustard

1 cup honey

½ cup mayonnaise

1 teaspoon lemon juice

1. In a small bowl, combine all honey mustard marinade ingredients. Use an electric mixer to whip the mixture for about 30 seconds. Place chicken in a resealable plastic bag and pour in about one-third of the marinade. Refrigerate for about 2 hours. Chill the remaining marinade until later.

2. Heat the oven to 375 degrees F.

3. In a small frying pan, sauté the mushrooms in the butter for 5–7 minutes, until mushrooms are golden brown. Set aside.

4. After the chicken has marinated, remove chicken from bag and discard the marinade. In an ovenproof frying pan, heat chicken and oil over medium heat. Sear the chicken in the pan for 3–4 minutes per side, or until golden brown. Remove pan from heat but keep chicken in the pan.

5. Brush each seared chicken breast with a little of the honey mustard marinade, being sure to save a little extra that you can serve on the side later. Season the chicken with salt, pepper, and paprika. Stack 2 pieces of cooked bacon crosswise on each chicken breast. Spoon the sautéed mushrooms onto the bacon, being sure to coat each breast evenly. Sprinkle ¼ cup Monterey Jack cheese evenly onto each breast followed by ¼ cup cheddar.

6. Bake the pan of prepared chicken breasts for 7–10 minutes, or until cheese is thoroughly melted and starting to bubble. Sprinkle each breast with ½ teaspoon parsley before serving. Put extra honey mustard marinade into a small bowl to serve on the side.

NOTE

If you don't have an ovenproof frying pan, you can sear the chicken over the stove in a frying pan and then transfer it to a baking dish for the oven.

TERIYAKI CHICKEN

Inspired by Mo'Bettahs

PREP TIME: 15 MIN · COOK TIME: 20 MIN · MARINATE TIME: 4 HOURS
TOTAL TIME: 4 HOURS 35 MIN · SERVES 5

This chicken is tender and flavorful and goes great with any Hawaiian dish. Pair it with grilled pineapple spears and our Hawaiian Macaroni Salad on page 135.

1½ pounds boneless skinless chicken thighs

1 cup soy sauce

1 cup brown sugar

1 cup pineapple juice

4 cloves garlic, chopped

1 tablespoon minced fresh ginger

1. Place chicken thighs in a bowl or large resealable plastic bag. Set aside.

2. Combine remaining ingredients in a medium-sized mixing bowl and mix until sugar dissolves. Pour marinade over chicken and seal tightly.

3. Refrigerate at least 4 hours or overnight.

4. Remove chicken from bag and set aside. Do not discard marinade. Pour marinade in a medium saucepan. Bring to a simmer. Cook for 5–10 minutes.

5. Pour some of the hot marinade in a separate bowl. Place chicken on grill and brush some of the hot marinade from the separate bowl over the top. Do not place brush back in main bowl of marinade after brushing the chicken. Grill chicken until it reaches an internal temperature of 165 degrees F.

6. Place cooked chicken in a baking dish and pour remaining hot teriyaki marinade over the top. Serve immediately.

CHICKEN MADEIRA

Inspired by The Cheesecake Factory

PREP TIME: 20 MIN · COOK TIME: 35 MIN · MARINATE TIME: 2 HOURS
TOTAL TIME: 2 HOURS 55 MIN · SERVES 4

The Cheesecake Factory's chicken Madeira has everything you need—chicken, asparagus, cheese, and mushrooms, not to mention the incredible sauce that tops it all!

4 boneless skinless chicken
   breasts

Marinade

¾ cup balsamic vinegar

½ cup olive oil

2 teaspoons brown sugar

pepper, to taste

Sauce

3 tablespoons butter or oil

2 cups fresh white mushrooms,
   sliced

1 cup balsamic vinegar

1 cup beef broth

2 tablespoons brown sugar

pepper, to taste

Topping

1 tablespoon butter or oil

12 spears asparagus

4 slices provolone cheese

4 slices mozzarella cheese

fresh parsley, for garnish

1. Place chicken breasts between two pieces of plastic wrap or waxed paper and pound until about ½-inch thick.

2. Place chicken in a resealable plastic bag. Combine marinade ingredients and pour in the bag. Squeeze all the air out, seal, and refrigerate for about 2 hours.

3. About 20 minutes before chicken is done marinating, heat butter or oil in a large skillet. Add mushrooms and sauté for a couple minutes. Add remaining sauce ingredients and bring to a boil. Reduce heat and simmer, uncovered, for about 30 minutes, or until sauce thickens and reduces to about ½–¼ of its original volume. When it is done, the sauce should be dark brown in color. Set aside.

4. While the mushrooms simmer, cook the chicken. Heat oven to 400 degrees F. Grease a 9x13-inch baking dish. Place chicken in dish and bake for 15–20 minutes, or until chicken is cooked through. Set aside.

5. While chicken is baking, sauté the asparagus spears in some butter or oil until bright green and crisp-tender, about 5–7 minutes. Set aside.

6. Once chicken and asparagus have cooked, layer on each chicken 1 slice provolone cheese, 3 cooked asparagus spears, then 1 slice mozzarella cheese. Set the oven to broil. Bake for about 3 minutes, or until the cheese melts and browns a little.

7. Right before serving, spoon some of the sauce over each piece of chicken. Garnish with fresh parsley and serve with mashed potatoes.

NOTE

Buy provolone and mozzarella cheese by the slice at your grocery store deli counter. The cheese melts better and is less expensive than buying pre-packaged cheese.

HONEY BAKED HAM

Inspired by **The Honey Baked Ham Company**

PREP TIME: 10 MIN · COOK TIME: 5 HOURS · TOTAL TIME: 5 HOURS 10 MIN · SERVES 15

Honey Baked Ham is a Christmas and Easter tradition everyone looks forward to! Sweet, smoky, and with succulent spices, this copycat recipe tastes just like your favorite holiday ham but is made right at home.

1 (8-to-10-pound) fully cooked bone-in spiral sliced ham

1 cup honey

½ cup brown sugar

5 tablespoons butter

2 tablespoons spicy brown mustard

1 teaspoon cinnamon

1 teaspoon nutmeg

1 teaspoon ground cloves

1 teaspoon paprika

1. Heat oven to 200 degrees F. Line a roasting pan with foil or a roasting pan liner. Place ham in prepared pan. Set aside.

2. In a small saucepan, combine all remaining ingredients. Heat over medium-low until sugar is just dissolved. You do not need to bring it to a boil.

3. Baste ham with about one-third of the honey mixture. Be sure to get in between all the slices.

4. Cover and bake for 5 hours, basting a second time halfway through using half of the remaining honey mixture. Check the temperature often. When the ham reaches 140 degrees F., it is ready.

5. Remove ham from oven and set oven to broil. While oven is getting to temperature, baste ham one last time using remaining mixture. Be sure to get a nice even coating over the top.

6. Place ham, uncovered, back in the oven. Watch it closely! When the glaze starts to caramelize and bubble up, remove ham from oven. Allow ham to rest for 5 minutes before serving.

NOTES

• Save yourself some cleanup time and line your roasting pan. That glorious honey and brown sugar mixture is delicious, but it makes a sticky mess! If you line your pan, then all you have to do is toss the liner out afterward.

• Use a heavy-duty roasting pan if you can. We love the Magnalite roasting pan. Cover the ham with foil or a lid when cooking. You want to keep all those juices in the ham.

• When basting, use a silicone basting brush. The honey mixture is sticky, and you don't want little stringy fibers getting into your baste from other types of brushes.

MAIN DISHES

MUSHROOM CHICKEN

Inspired by Panda Express

PREP TIME: 5 MIN · COOK TIME: 15 MIN · TOTAL TIME: 20 MIN · SERVES 4

This Panda Express mushroom chicken made at home tastes even better than the restaurant's popular dish! Plus the tender chicken, hearty mushrooms, and signature sauce are done faster than you can get takeout.

2 pounds boneless skinless chicken thighs or breasts

⅓ cup cornstarch

5 tablespoons olive oil, divided

1 cup white mushrooms, sliced

2 tablespoons soy sauce

2 large zucchini, cut into ½-inch pieces

Ginger Soy Sauce

1 cup chicken broth

¼ cup soy sauce

2 tablespoons white cooking wine

2 tablespoons rice vinegar

2 teaspoons crushed garlic

2 teaspoons grated or finely chopped fresh ginger

1 teaspoon brown sugar

3 tablespoons cornstarch

¼ cup water

1. Cut chicken into bite-size pieces and toss in cornstarch until each piece is well coated. Set aside.

2. Heat 3 tablespoons olive oil over medium heat in a large skillet or wok. Add chicken pieces to skillet one at a time, spacing them apart far enough that they aren't touching. Cook for 5–6 minutes per side, or until the outside of the chicken is golden brown and it is cooked through all the way. Remove cooked chicken from skillet, cover, and set aside.

3. Wipe skillet clean. Place skillet back on stovetop over medium-high heat and add remaining 2 tablespoons oil. Add mushrooms and soy sauce. Sauté for about 1 minute. Add zucchini and sauté until the zucchini is just cooked through. Do not overcook; the zucchini should still have some bite to it.

4. Add chicken back to the skillet and stir in the ginger soy sauce until chicken and veggies are all covered in sauce. Serve immediately with rice or chow mein (see page 125).

Ginger Soy Sauce

1. Combine chicken broth, soy sauce, white wine, rice vinegar, garlic, ginger, and brown sugar in a small saucepan. Bring to simmer. Cook for about 5 minutes, stirring often.

2. In a small bowl, stir cornstarch and water together. Slowly add mixture to the sauce, whisking constantly until sauce thickens. You may not need all of the cornstarch mixture. Remove from heat and set aside until ready to use.

NOTE

Feel free to add additional ingredients! Here are some ideas.

- broccoli
- green bell pepper
- carrots
- diced onions or a sprinkle of onion powder
- green beans
- fresh parsley, fresh thyme, or other fresh herbs
- sesame seeds

MAIN DISHES

COPYCAT SATU'LI BOWLS

Inspired by **Satu'li Canteen,** *Pandora—The World of Avatar, Disney's Animal Kingdom*

PREP TIME: 1 HOUR 15 MIN · COOK TIME: 5 HOURS · MARINATE TIME: OVERNIGHT
TOTAL TIME: 6 HOURS 15 MIN PLUS OVERNIGHT · MAKES 6 BOWLS

Step out of reality and into Pandora—The World of Avatar with these delicious bowls inspired by the Satu'li Canteen in Disney's Animal Kingdom at Walt Disney World.

20 ounces lo mein noodles

1 tablespoon olive oil

¾ cup juicy popping boba balls, for garnish

Slow-Roasted Beef

3 pounds beef roast (you won't use ALL the roast, but to make it work for slicing you will want to make the full amount and just use as much as you need)

½ cup olive oil

¼ cup red wine vinegar

3 tablespoons minced fresh garlic

1 tablespoon Italian seasoning

2 teaspoons dried rosemary

1 teaspoon dried thyme

1 teaspoon onion powder

½ teaspoon red pepper flakes

kosher salt and pepper, to taste

Grilled Canteen Chicken

2 pounds boneless skinless chicken thighs or breasts

¼ cup canola oil

3 tablespoons apple cider vinegar

3 tablespoons minced fresh garlic

kosher salt and pepper, to taste

Slow-Roasted Beef

1. Place beef roast in a resealable plastic bag. In a medium-sized mixing bowl, whisk together all remaining roast ingredients until well combined. Pour mixture over the roast and seal the bag, pressing out as much air as you can. Marinate in the refrigerator overnight.

2. Remove beef from bag and discard excess marinade. Place roast in a roasting pan. Roast, uncovered, at 200 degrees F. for 3-4 hours or until internal temperature reaches 130 degrees F. Remove from oven and cover with foil. Allow to rest for 30-40 minutes.

3. Using a sharp carving knife, slice into very thin slices to serve over your noodle bowls.

Grilled Canteen Chicken

1. Place chicken thighs in a large resealable plastic bag. In a small mixing bowl, whisk together all remaining chicken ingredients. Pour mixture over the chicken and seal the bag, pressing out as much air as you can. Marinate in the refrigerator overnight.

2. Remove chicken from bag and discard excess marinade. Grill over medium heat until chicken is completely cooked through, reaching a temperature of 165 degrees F. Remove from grill and cover with foil. Allow to rest 10-15 minutes.

3. Cut chicken into cubes and serve over noodle bowls.

CONTINUED ON NEXT PAGE

MAIN DISHES

COPYCAT SATU'LI BOWLS

CONTINUED

Crunchy Slaw

1 cup matchstick carrots

1 cup shredded cabbage

3 tablespoons olive oil

3 tablespoons distilled white
    vinegar

kosher salt and pepper, to taste

Creamy Herb Dressing

1 cup mayonnaise

¼ cup water

¼ cup lemon juice

¼ teaspoon ground sumac (see
    recipe notes)

¼ teaspoon ground cardamom

⅛ teaspoon ground turmeric

kosher salt and pepper, to taste

Crunchy Slaw

1. Place the matchstick carrots and shredded cabbage in a medium-sized mixing bowl. Set aside.

2. In a small mixing bowl, whisk together oil, vinegar, salt, and pepper. Toss mixture with the carrot-cabbage mixture until well coated. Serve immediately over the noodle bowls.

Creamy Herb Dressing

1. Combine all dressing ingredients in a blender or food processor. Pulse or blend until well combined. Cover and refrigerate overnight.

Assembly

1. Cook lo mein noodles according to package directions. Drain well and allow to cool. Toss in olive oil and refrigerate until ready to eat. You can serve the lo mein noodles warm, but they are served cold at Disney's Animal Kingdom.

2. Divide lo mein noodles among 6 pasta serving bowls. Add about ½ cup beef and ½ cup chicken to each bowl, or just divide evenly. Add slaw to each bowl and top each with about 2 tablespoons boba balls. Serve with ¼ cup creamy herb dressing per bowl.

NOTES

• The beef, the chicken, and the dressing should be made the night before so they can sit overnight. The slaw and lo mein can be prepared right before assembling.

• When you first make the creamy herb dressing, it will have no color to it. After it sets you will notice the natural color from the spices will make it look light green, just like in the park. You can serve it on the side or drizzle it over the meat.

• You can find ground sumac in a small packet at any Asian market. If you can't find sumac, lemon zest is a decent substitute.

THAI CHICKEN PIZZA

Inspired by California Pizza Kitchen

PREP TIME: 45 MIN · RISING TIME: 1 HOUR AND 45 MIN · COOK TIME: 15 MIN
TOTAL TIME: 2 HOURS AND 45 MIN · SERVES 8

This Thai chicken pizza is just like the one at California Pizza Kitchen. You will love it! The peanut sauce is soooo good!

2 boneless skinless chicken breasts

¾ cup House of Tsang Bangkok Peanut Sauce (for the marinade)

Dough

1½ cups warm water

2 tablespoons sugar

1 (.25-ounce) packet active dry yeast

3¾ cups flour

1 tablespoon kosher salt

3 tablespoons olive oil

Peanut Sauce

½ cup chicken broth

4 cloves garlic, pressed or minced

6 heaping tablespoons creamy peanut butter

6 tablespoons soy sauce

3 tablespoons honey

3 tablespoons minced fresh ginger

2–4 teaspoons sriracha sauce, to taste

1. Place chicken in a resealable bag and add Tsang Bangkok Peanut Sauce. Marinate in the refrigerator for at least 1 hour while the dough is prepared and rising. The chicken can also be marinated and grilled ahead of time.

2. Prepare pizza dough by combining water, sugar, and yeast in a small bowl. Let sit 5 minutes.

3. Mix flour and salt together in the bowl of a heavy-duty mixer fitted with a dough hook.

4. Add oil to the yeast mixture, then pour yeast mixture into the flour mixture. Knead on low speed for 10 minutes.

5. Place dough in a lightly oiled bowl. Turn the dough over a few times to coat the dough with oil. Cover with plastic wrap and let rise in a warm place for 1 hour.

6. Punch the dough down and divide in half. Shape into 2 balls. Lightly brush the dough balls with olive oil and return them to the bowl. Cover again with plastic wrap, and let rise another 45 minutes.

7. While the dough is rising the second time, stir together all the sauce ingredients in a saucepan and simmer on low heat for 10 minutes. Set aside.

8. Once sauce is prepared, remove the chicken from the refrigerator and discard the excess marinade. Heat barbecue grill to 400 degrees F. Grill the chicken for 7 minutes on each side, only turning once. Use a meat thermometer to make sure the internal temperature of the chicken reaches 165 degrees F. Allow chicken to sit for 10 minutes, then cut into thin slices.

9. Heat oven to 450 degrees F.

10. Lightly grease a pizza pan or dust it with cornmeal.

11. Take one dough ball and place it in the center of the pizza

CONTINUED ON NEXT PAGE

MAIN DISHES

171

THAI CHICKEN PIZZA

CONTINUED

Toppings

3 cups mozzarella cheese

½ cup julienned carrots

½ cup bean sprouts

½ cup whole peanuts

¼ cup chopped fresh cilantro

¼ cup diced green onion

pan. Using your fingers, pat the dough out from the center to the edge of the pan, with the dough slightly thicker on the rim of the pizza pan. See recipe notes for what to do with remaining dough ball.

12. Top the dough with the prepared peanut sauce, cheese, grilled chicken slices, carrots, bean sprouts, peanuts, cilantro, and green onion. Bake for 10–15 minutes, until the edges are golden brown.

NOTE

This is the only homemade pizza dough recipe we ever use. It is so easy to prepare, and, unlike some dough recipes we have tried, it actually tastes delicious! It makes enough dough for two large pizzas. You can make two pizzas, make one and freeze one, or use the second to make breadsticks instead. The dough keeps great in the freezer; just be sure to bring the dough to room temperature again before rolling it out. If you want to use a store-bought pizza crust or use another homemade version (like a cauliflower pizza crust), that is totally fine too!

STEAK

Inspired by Chipotle

PREP TIME: 10 MIN · COOK TIME: 20 MIN · MARINATE TIME: 30 MIN
TOTAL TIME: 1 HOUR · SERVES 8

Discover the secret to making Chipotle steak at home! Our recipe gives you juicy and flavorful bites of steak for a salad, bowl, or burrito.

2 pounds top sirloin steak

2 tablespoons neutral oil like canola or avocado

Marinade

4 ounces chipotle peppers in adobo sauce (about half of a 7-ounce can)

1 teaspoon cumin

1 teaspoon dried oregano

1 teaspoon salt

1 teaspoon pepper

½ red onion, chopped

4 cloves garlic, peeled

juice of 2 limes

1. Add all marinade ingredients to a blender. Blend until it reaches a saucy consistency.

2. Add steak and marinade to a resealable plastic bag or lidded container and shake around until the steak is coated. Refrigerate for at least 30 minutes or up to 12 hours.

3. Heat oil in a cast-iron skillet over medium-high heat. Depending on the size of your skillet, you may have to cook in batches. Add the steak and cook until the internal temperature reaches 140 degrees F, flipping once. Move the steak to a cutting board and cover with foil. Let rest for 10 minutes.

4. Chop steak into bite-size pieces. Serve in bowls, tacos, salads, or burritos!

NOTES

• If you want the steak spicier, add the whole can of peppers to the marinade. You can use this marinade on chicken or pork as well.

• Store leftover steak in an airtight container in the fridge. Reheat in a skillet for best results.

SEASONED TACO BEEF

Inspired by Taco Bell

PREP TIME: 15 MIN · COOK TIME: 35 MIN · TOTAL TIME: 50 MIN · SERVES 16

This Taco Bell meat recipe tastes just like the real deal. The texture and flavor is spot-on, plus it's *so* easy to make!

2 pounds ground beef (85% lean, 15% fat)

2⅓ cups water or beef broth, divided

5 tablespoons taco seasoning (homemade or store-bought), or to taste

2 tablespoons cornstarch

1 teaspoon unsweetened cocoa powder, for color (optional)

salt, to taste

1. Combine ground beef, 1⅔ cups water, taco seasoning, cornstarch, and cocoa powder in a mixing bowl. Mix by hand or with a mixer until all the ingredients are fully incorporated. It should be sticky and almost like a thick batter.

2. Grease a large nonstick skillet or Dutch oven with cooking oil. Add the meat mixture. Pour the remaining ⅔ cup water in, cover, and cook on medium-high heat for 5 minutes.

3. Use a spatula to break up the meat completely. Allow to simmer on low heat, uncovered, until the water evaporates and the meat mixture thickens, 20–30 minutes. Taste along the way and season with salt if needed.

4. Serve with hard or soft taco shells, or use it to create your favorite Taco Bell item!

NOTE

You can also easily cook the Taco Bell meat in a pressure cooker. Place ⅔ cup water in the pressure cooker and add the meat mixture. Seal and cook on high pressure for 7 minutes, then allow for a 10-minute natural release. Release the rest of the pressure with a quick release and use a metal spatula to break up the meat. Switch the setting to sauté and cook until the meat mixture thickens.

MAIN DISHES

COPYCAT IMPOSSIBLE SPOONFUL

Inspired by **Pym Test Kitchen**, *Avengers Campus, Disney California Adventure Park*

PREP TIME: 20 MIN · COOK TIME: 15 MIN · TOTAL TIME: 35 MIN · SERVES 3

This copycat Impossible Spoonful recipe will transport you right back to Avengers Campus. Plus, it is completely plant-based!

6 ounces penne pasta

6 ounces mini penne pasta

1½ cups spaghetti sauce

dairy-free Parmesan cheese, for serving

microgreens, for serving

Impossible Meatballs

1 (12-ounce) package Impossible ground beef

¼ cup diced onion

3 cloves garlic, minced

2 tablespoons dairy-free Parmesan cheese

3 teaspoons Italian seasoning

2 tablespoons bread crumbs

1 teaspoon salt

red pepper flakes, to taste

1. Heat oven to 425 degrees F. Combine all meatball ingredients in a bowl. Mix until fully combined.

2. Roll out 3 large meatballs and 6 small meatballs. Place on a baking sheet. Bake for 10 minutes, then remove the small meatballs. Bake the larger meatballs for 5 more minutes, or until the internal temperature reaches 165 degrees F.

3. While the meatballs are cooking, cook the pastas according to package directions. Drain. Place the pasta back in the pot and stir the spaghetti sauce in with the pasta.

4. Serve by adding pasta to each bowl and then topping with 1 large meatball and 2 small meatballs. Top with Parmesan and microgreens.

DESSERTS

CHOCOLATE BUNDT CAKE

Inspired by Nothing Bundt Cakes

PREP TIME: 20 MIN · BAKE TIME: 50 MIN · COOL TIME: 20 MIN · CHILL TIME: OVERNIGHT
TOTAL TIME: 1 HOUR 30 MIN PLUS OVERNIGHT · SERVES 16

This chocolate Bundt cake is rich, moist, and delicious! Our easy-to-make recipe is a close replica of the popular Chocolate Chocolate Chip Bundt Cake from Nothing Bundt Cakes.

Chocolate Cake

1 (15.25-ounce) box devil's food cake mix

1 (3.4-ounce) package instant chocolate pudding mix

1 cup sour cream

4 large eggs

½ cup water

½ cup oil

1½ cups mini chocolate chips

Cream Cheese Frosting

16 ounces cream cheese, softened

½ cup butter, softened

2 teaspoons vanilla extract

3–4 cups powdered sugar

Chocolate Cake

1. Heat oven to 350 degrees F. Grease a standard Bundt cake pan. Set aside.

2. Mix together cake mix, pudding mix, sour cream, eggs, water, and oil. Stir in chocolate chips. Pour into prepared pan.

3. Bake for 45–50 minutes. Remove from oven. Let cool for 20 minutes.

4. Remove cake from Bundt pan by placing a plate upside down over the Bundt pan. While holding the plate firmly on top, flip both over so the cake comes out onto the plate. Cover the cake with plastic wrap and place it in the fridge overnight before frosting.

Cream Cheese Frosting

1. In a medium bowl, cream together cream cheese and butter until creamy. Mix in the vanilla, then gradually stir in the powdered sugar. Start with 2 cups, then keep adding more until it is nice and thick.

2. Spoon the frosting into a resealable zip-top gallon bag. Clip one bottom corner of the bag. Squeeze frosting out of the bag onto the cake in strips, as pictured.

WHITE CHOCOLATE RASPBERRY BUNDT CAKE

Inspired by Nothing Bundt Cakes

PREP TIME: 10 MIN · BAKE TIME: 50 MIN · COOL TIME: 20 MIN · CHILL TIME: OVERNIGHT
TOTAL TIME: 1 HOUR 20 MIN PLUS OVERNIGHT · SERVES 16

This white chocolate raspberry cake copycat tastes just like the popular Nothing Bundt Cakes bakery version! It's creamy, flavorful, and easy to make at home.

White Chocolate Raspberry Cake

1 (15.25-ounce) box white cake mix

1 (3.4-ounce) package instant white chocolate pudding mix

1 cup sour cream

4 large eggs

¼ cup water

½ cup oil

1 cup white chocolate chips, chopped into smaller pieces

½ cup red raspberry preserves, divided

Cream Cheese Frosting

16 ounces cream cheese, softened

½ cup butter, softened

2 teaspoons vanilla extract

3–4 cups powdered sugar

White Chocolate Raspberry Cake

1. Heat oven to 350 degrees F. Grease a standard Bundt pan with cooking spray. Set aside.

2. Mix together cake mix, pudding mix, sour cream, eggs, water, and oil. Fold in white chocolate chips.

3. Fill prepared pan with half of the batter. Spoon ¼ cup raspberry preserves in 5 or 6 small spoonfuls over the batter. Using a knife, swirl the filling through the cake thoroughly, do not leave large clumps of preserves in the batter. Pour remaining batter in evenly. Spoon remaining ¼ cup raspberry preserves onto batter, repeating the swirling process.

4. Bake for 45–50 minutes. Remove from oven. Let cool for 10 minutes.

5. Remove cake from Bundt pan by placing a plate upside down over the Bundt pan. While holding the plate firmly on top, flip both over so the cake comes out onto the plate. Cover the cake with plastic wrap and place it in the fridge overnight before frosting.

Cream Cheese Frosting

1. In a medium bowl, cream together cream cheese and butter until creamy. Mix in the vanilla, then gradually stir in the powdered sugar. Start with 2 cups, then keep adding more until it is nice and thick.

2. Spoon the frosting into a resealable zip-top gallon bag. Clip one bottom corner of the bag. Squeeze frosting out of the bag onto the cake in strips, as pictured.

CHOCOLATE MELTING CAKE

Inspired by Carnival Cruise Line

PREP TIME: 15 MIN · COOK TIME: 14 MIN · TOTAL TIME: 29 MIN · SERVES 4

If you have been on a Carnival cruise, you've probably had this warm chocolate melting cake, and you know how amazingly good it is!

¾ cup dark chocolate chips

¾ cup butter

4 eggs, room temperature

¾ cup sugar

⅛ teaspoon vanilla extract

¼ cup flour

powdered sugar, for dusting

ice cream, for serving

whipped cream, for serving

1. Heat oven to 375 degrees F.

2. Melt chocolate chips and butter in a small saucepan. Set aside to cool for 10 minutes.

3. In a separate bowl, whisk eggs and sugar together. Add vanilla and flour. Whisk until flour is well mixed in. Once chocolate has cooled, combine with egg mixture.

4. Fill 4 (7-ounce) ramekins about three-fourths full with chocolate batter. Bake for 14 minutes. Check to make sure the edges of the cakes are cooked and the top of the cakes appear to be cooked as well. See recipe notes.

5. Once cooled, sprinkle cakes lightly with powdered sugar. Serve with ice cream or whipped cream.

NOTES

• You'll need 4 (7-ounce) ramekins to make these, not a regular cake pan.

• Watch these babies closely. Do not overbake! The cake is supposed to be spongy and cakey on top but gooey and melty in the middle—the consistency of pudding, not too runny. If you put the toothpick all the way down to the bottom and the bottom half of the toothpick *doesn't* come out clean, you did it right.

APPLE PIE CARAMEL APPLES

Inspired by Disneyland

PREP TIME: 20 MIN · CHILL TIME: 2 HOURS · TOTAL TIME: 2 HOURS 20 MIN · SERVES 4

Disneyland's apple pie caramel apples are my new favorite treat! Now you can bring the magic to your kitchen with this easy recipe.

4 caramel apple sticks or popsicle sticks

4 large Granny Smith apples, washed and chilled

5 cups caramels, unwrapped, or about 1 bag Kraft Caramel Bits

7 cinnamon graham crackers

1½ pounds melting chocolates or chocolate chips

2 tablespoons sugar

⅛ teaspoon ground cinnamon

8 large marshmallows for Mickey ears (optional)

1. Prepare a plate or tray by covering it with a sheet of waxed paper. Place a stick in the top of each apple. Set aside.

2. If using unwrapped caramel squares, place them in a microwave-safe dish. Microwave in 30-second intervals, stirring in between, until the caramel is nice and melted. You can also put the caramels in a small slow cooker on high heat and cook until melted. If using the Bits, follow the directions on the package.

3. Dip each apple into the caramel, rotating as needed, until fully coated. Let excess caramel drip off, then place the apples on the waxed paper. Refrigerate for at least 2 hours, until caramel is completely cooled.

4. While apples chill, prepare graham crackers, chocolate, and cinnamon sugar. In a food processor, process graham crackers or pie crust (see notes) until well blended. Place crushed crackers in a bowl and set aside.

5. In a microwave-safe dish, microwave chocolate in 30-second intervals, stirring in between, until chocolate is just melted and there are no lumps. Set aside.

6. In a small bowl, combine sugar and cinnamon. Set aside.

7. Once the caramel has cooled, dip each apple in the chocolate, rotating as needed, until fully coated. Allow the chocolate to set up for a few seconds. When the chocolate has set a little, roll the bottom half in processed graham cracker crumbs. Sprinkle the entire apple with cinnamon sugar and set aside on the tray on the counter to cool, about 10 minutes. The chocolate will be set when it's no longer shiny.

8. Once the chocolate on the apples has set, cut each marshmallow in half. Roll each marshmallow half in the chocolate and place on the apples to make Mickey ears. Sprinkle with cinnamon and sugar and hold in place until set.

NOTES

- Don't skip on the washing and refrigerating of the apples before dipping! Washing gets the wax coating from the food companies off. If you *really* want to get the wax off, drop the apples in boiling water for a few seconds and wipe dry; otherwise, just rinse and wipe with a dishcloth or paper towel. Then chill the apples in the refrigerator. This will really help the caramel to stick to the apples.

- You can use a prepared graham cracker pie crust in place of the graham crackers. Process it in the food processor the same way and add some extra cinnamon and sugar (about ½ teaspoon each) to the crumbs.

- Refrigerate the apples when setting up the caramel, but let the chocolate set up at room temperature.

FUDGE

Inspired by See's Candies

PREP TIME: 10 MIN · COOK TIME: 10 MIN · CHILL TIME: OVERNIGHT
TOTAL TIME: 20 MIN PLUS OVERNIGHT · MAKES 60 PIECES

This See's fudge recipe is the easiest, most foolproof fudge recipe ever! It never gets grainy and comes out perfectly every time.

16 ounces milk chocolate

24 ounces semisweet chocolate chips

½ cup butter

1 (7-ounce) jar marshmallow creme

4¼ cups sugar

1 (12-ounce) can evaporated milk

1 teaspoon vanilla

1. Butter a 9x13-inch glass baking dish. Set aside.

2. Combine milk chocolate, chocolate chips, butter, and marshmallow in a large mixing bowl. Set aside.

3. In a large saucepan, combine sugar and evaporated milk. Bring to a rolling boil over medium heat. Stir constantly at the rolling boil for 4 minutes with a wooden spoon.

4. Remove from heat and stir in vanilla.

5. Pour evaporated milk mixture over chocolate mixture in several intervals, stirring constantly to keep the fudge from clumping. Continue stirring until well blended and smooth.

6. Pour into prepared baking dish. Cover tightly and refrigerate several hours or overnight, until hardened. Keep refrigerated until you serve.

NOTE

For the milk chocolate, use 2 giant (7.56-ounce) Hershey bars and break them into pieces. For the chocolate chips, we like the Guittard brand.

CHOCOLATE SATIN PIE

Inspired by **Marie Callender's**

PREP TIME: 20 MIN · BAKE TIME: 10 MIN · CHILL TIME: 2 HOURS
TOTAL TIME: 2 HOURS 30 MIN · SERVES 8

This Marie Callender's chocolate satin pie copycat recipe is spot-on! The pie is rich and creamy, just like the chocolate satin pie at the restaurant.

Cookie Crust

18 OREO sandwich cookies, halved, with middles scraped out (36 chocolate cookies total)

½ cup butter, melted

Filling

2 tablespoons water

1 (.25-ounce) package unflavored gelatin

1 large egg

½ cup whole or 2% milk

4 tablespoons sugar

⅓ cup unsweetened cocoa powder

1 cup semisweet chocolate chips

2 cups plus 2 tablespoons heavy whipping cream, divided

Topping

2 cups minus 2 tablespoons heavy whipping cream (see note)

2 tablespoons sugar

1 chocolate bar (regular-size), grated

Cookie Crust

1. Heat oven to 325 degrees F.

2. Place the cookies in a food processor or blender and blend into fine crumbs. Add melted better to the crumbs and stir well.

3. Press mixture into a 9-inch or 9.5-inch pie plate. Bake for 10 minutes. Allow to cool before adding filling.

Filling

1. Place water in a mixing bowl. Sprinkle gelatin over water. Set aside.

2. Whisk egg, milk, sugar, and cocoa powder in a small saucepan until smooth. Heat on low, stirring constantly, until mixture is slightly thickened. Add mixture to gelatin and stir until smooth. Set aside.

3. Place chocolate chips and 2 tablespoons heavy whipping cream in a microwave-safe dish. Heat in the microwave at 50 percent power for 30 seconds. Stir. Heat at 50 percent power in additional 10-second increments, stirring well between each set, until chocolate is smooth. Add to the bowl with the gelatin mixture. Stir well.

4. Beat 2 cups heavy whipping cream in a mixer or large bowl until stiff. Gently fold whipped cream into the chocolate mixture. You have to sneak a taste at this point—it is delicious!

5. Pour completed filling into cookie crust and refrigerate for 2 hours, or until set.

Topping

1. Beat remaining whipping cream and sugar until stiff. Use to decorate the top of the pie.

2. Sprinkle with grated chocolate.

NOTES

- Use the Knox brand of unflavored gelatin.

- If you buy 1 quart of heavy whipping cream, you will have enough for this whole recipe. Use 2 cups plus 2 tablespoons for the filling and the remaining cream (which is slightly less than 2 cups) for the topping.

- This chocolate satin pie needs to be placed in the refrigerator when storing. It is best to lightly wrap this pie or use an airtight container that does not touch the topping. Place in the fridge for 5-7 days or in the freezer for 1 month. When ready to enjoy the frozen pie, let thaw in the refrigerator overnight.

MAPLE BUTTER BLONDIES

Inspired by **Applebee's**

PREP TIME: 10 MIN · COOK TIME: 25 MIN · TOTAL TIME: 35 MIN · SERVES 9

Applebee's maple butter blondie dessert is topped with ice cream and maple butter sauce. This buttery brownie has a flaky top and a gooey center—delicious!

Blondies

½ cup (1 stick) butter, melted

1 cup brown sugar

1 large egg

1½ teaspoons vanilla extract

⅛ teaspoon salt

1 cup flour

1½ cups butterscotch chips

Maple Butter Sauce

⅓ cup butter

1 cup sugar

8 ounces cream cheese, softened

¼ cup pure maple syrup

2 tablespoons brown sugar

Toppings

butter pecan ice cream

chopped candied pecans

Blondies

1. Heat oven to 350 degrees F. Grease an 8x8-inch baking dish. Set aside.

2. In a large bowl, combine butter and brown sugar. Mix until smooth.

3. Add egg, vanilla, and salt. Stir until blended.

4. Mix in flour until combined. Fold in butterscotch chips.

5. Spread the batter into the baking dish. Bake for 25 minutes.

Maple Butter Sauce

1. In a medium saucepan over medium heat, combine all maple butter sauce ingredients. Stir until smooth. Simmer for 10–15 minutes, stirring frequently.

2. Once the blondies are cooked and cooled completely, cut into squares, plate with ice cream, sprinkle with chopped pecans, and drizzle sauce over the top.

ASPHALT PIE

Inspired by **Wingers**

PREP TIME: 25 MIN · FREEZE TIME: 3 HOURS · TOTAL TIME: 3 HOURS 25 MIN · SERVES 8

This Asphalt Pie is *amazing*! The chocolate mint ice cream drizzled with caramel and sprinkled with cookies is to die for.

Asphalt Pie

24 OREO cookies, crushed

¼ cup butter, melted

1½ quarts mint chocolate chip ice cream

Salted Caramel Topping

½ cup sugar

3 tablespoons butter, sliced

¼ cup heavy whipping cream

½ teaspoon sea salt

Whipped Cream

1 cup whipping cream

½ cup powdered sugar

Asphalt Pie

1. In a small bowl, mix crushed cookies and melted butter. Stir until combined.

2. Press crust into the bottom of a 9-inch pie plate. Fill with ice cream. Cover and freeze for at least 3 hours before serving.

Salted Caramel Topping

1. Heat the sugar in a saucepan over medium heat, stirring constantly and scraping the bottom, until the sugar has melted into an amber liquid, about 2–3 minutes.

2. Once the sugar has melted, add the butter. Once the butter has melted, add the cream. Boil for 1 minute. Remove from heat and stir in sea salt.

Whipped Cream

1. Using an electric mixer, beat cream and powdered sugar until stiff peaks form.

2. Remove pie from freezer. Drizzle caramel topping over each slice and add whipped cream.

NOTE

Double the amount of ice cream for a mile-high pie!

PUMPKIN PASTIES

Inspired by The Wizarding World of Harry Potter

PREP TIME: 15 MIN · COOK TIME: 30 MIN · TOTAL TIME: 45 MIN · SERVES 12

Bring the magical world of Harry Potter into your own kitchen with these sweet and flavorful pumpkin pasties!

2 (14.1-ounce) Pillsbury
   refrigerated pie crusts

¾ cup pumpkin puree

3 ounces cream cheese, softened

⅓ cup sugar

2 teaspoons pumpkin pie spice

1 egg

¼ cup butter, melted

decorating sugar crystals,
   cinnamon sugar, or sprinkles
   (optional)

1. Heat oven to 350 degrees F.

2. Cut out 12 (4-inch) circles from the pie crusts using the top of a large cup, a cookie cutter, or a bowl, rerolling dough as needed. Set aside.

3. In a mixing bowl, combine the pumpkin puree, cream cheese, sugar, pumpkin pie spice, and egg. Set aside.

4. Using the rolling pin again, gently roll out each circle just a little more to create a crust slightly thinner than a regular pie crust. Evenly distribute the pumpkin filling between the 12 dough circles, placing the filling on one half of the circle. Gently fold the dough over the filling. Using a fork, press the edges of the dough together, sealing the filling inside.

5. Using a sharp knife, cut a few slits across the top of each pasty. Place each pasty on a baking sheet. Using a pastry brush, lightly coat each pasty with melted butter. Sprinkle the top of each pasty with sugar crystals, cinnamon sugar, or colored sugar sprinkles, if desired.

6. Bake for 25–30 minutes or until pasties are lightly browned.

HOMEMADE HULA PIE

Inspired by **Duke's**

PREP TIME: 15 MIN · FREEZE TIME: OVERNIGHT PLUS 1 HOUR
TOTAL TIME: 1 HOUR 15 MIN PLUS OVERNIGHT · SERVES 16

This hula pie is just like the original from Duke's without the expensive flight to the islands! It's like having a little slice of Hawaii in your home.

1 (9-inch) OREO pie crust, frozen (see note)

1 gallon French vanilla ice cream

2 teaspoons coconut extract

1¼ cups coarsely chopped macadamia nuts, divided

3 cups fudge topping (store-bought or homemade), divided

whipped cream, for topping

1. Remove ice cream from freezer and allow to soften for 10–15 minutes. You do *not* want it to melt, so keep a close eye on it. When the ice cream has softened, place it in a stand mixer bowl fitted with the dough hook attachment. Turn mixer to low and mix the ice cream until it reaches a thick frozen-yogurt consistency. Add coconut extract and 1 cup macadamia nuts. Mix for another minute.

2. Find a mixing bowl with a rim that will easily fit inside the pie crust. If using a 9-inch pie crust, find a bowl with a rim that is less than 9 inches. You will be placing the bowl upside down inside the crust after it's frozen.

3. Line the bowl with plastic wrap, spray with cooking spray, and scoop ice cream into the bowl. Cover with a lid or plastic wrap and freeze overnight.

4. Remove ice cream and crust from freezer. Remove cover from the ice cream bowl. Carefully place the bowl upside down in the crust. Pull the plastic wrap down until the ice cream settles onto the crust. Remove bowl and plastic wrap from ice cream.

5. Spoon 2 cups fudge topping over the ice cream dome. Do not heat the fudge; you don't want it to melt the ice cream. If you must heat to soften, do it for only a few seconds, until soft enough to remove from the container. Spread fudge evenly until ice cream is covered in fudge. Freeze again until fudge becomes firm, about 1 hour.

6. Remove from freezer and cut into slices using a warm knife. Top each slice with whipped cream, some of the remaining 1 cup hot fudge (it's okay for this fudge to be hot), and some of the remaining ¼ cup macadamia nuts.

NOTE

Put your pie crust in the pie plate you want to use and freeze it the same night you freeze the ice cream pie filling. You can use a store-bought or a homemade crust.

CHOCOLATE HAUPIA PIE

Inspired by **Ted's Bakery**

PREP TIME: 1 HOUR · CHILL TIME: 6 HOURS · TOTAL TIME: 7 HOURS · SERVES 8

Haupia is a coconut milk pudding, and chocolate haupia pie is a popular pie found in Hawaii. It's a rich chocolate pie with a coconut haupia layer and topped with whipped cream.

Chocolate Haupia Pie

1 (9-inch) pie crust (store-bought or homemade)

1½ cups whole milk, divided

5 tablespoons cornstarch

1 (14-ounce) can unsweetened coconut milk (not fat-free or light)

1 cup granulated sugar

1 cup semisweet chocolate chips

Whipped Cream

1½ cups heavy whipping cream

¼ cup sugar

½ teaspoon coconut extract (optional)

Chocolate Haupia Pie

1. Generously pierce crust with a fork. Bake according to recipe or according to package directions, until golden brown. Remove from oven and allow crust to cool.

2. In a liquid measuring cup or small bowl, combine ½ cup whole milk and cornstarch. Mix until cornstarch is dissolved. Set aside.

3. In a medium-sized saucepan over medium heat, whisk together remaining 1 cup whole milk, coconut milk, and sugar. Bring to a simmer, whisking often.

4. Stir cornstarch mixture once more before slowly adding to coconut milk mixture, whisking constantly. Continue whisking until mixture becomes thick, like a thick pudding. (This coconut milk pudding is the haupia.) It is very important that the mixture is thick before moving to the next step.

5. Place about half of the haupia mixture into a separate bowl and set aside. Add chocolate chips to the remaining mixture in the saucepan and stir until chocolate chips are completely melted and well combined.

6. Add chocolate haupia mixture immediately to cooled pie crust and smooth with a spatula until even. Add the remaining haupia mixture over the top and carefully smooth over until even.

7. Cover and refrigerate for 6 hours.

Whipped Cream

1. To make whipped cream, whip heavy cream and sugar until stiff peaks form. Add coconut extract and whip for 30 more seconds.

2. After pie has cooled, cut into slices and top with whipped cream topping. You can use a piping bag fitted with a large star tip to pipe the whipped cream in a design over the top.

CARAMEL APPLE BREAD PUDDING

Inspired by Epi's Basque Restaurant

PREP TIME: 10 MIN · SOAK TIME: OVERNIGHT · COOK TIME: 1 HOUR
TOTAL TIME: 1 HOUR 10 MIN PLUS OVERNIGHT · SERVES 12

The bread pudding at Epi's in Meridian, Idaho was a life-changing discovery. Let's just say the copycat recipe was essential to keep some money in the bank. The bread pudding is incredible all on its own, but add the creamy caramel sauce and you have *perfection*.

Bread Pudding

6 eggs

3 cups milk

3 cups heavy whipping cream

1 cup sugar

2 tablespoons vanilla extract

1 tablespoon cinnamon

12 croissants (regular size)

2 Granny Smith apples, sliced very thinly (about 2 cups)

whipped cream, for topping

Caramel Sauce

1½ cups heavy whipping cream, divided

1 cup sugar

1 cup light corn syrup

½ cup (1 stick) unsalted butter

Bread Pudding

1. Butter a 9x13-inch baking dish. Set aside.
2. Whisk eggs in a large bowl. Add milk, cream, sugar, vanilla, and cinnamon. Whisk together until frothy.
3. Tear croissants into bite-size pieces (about 1-inch cubes). Add to liquid mixture and stir gently until croissant pieces are soaked. Add sliced apples and stir to combine.
4. Pour mixture into prepared dish and allow to soak overnight.
5. When ready to bake, heat oven to 350 degrees F. Tightly cover the pan with foil and bake for 1 hour. Test for doneness by removing foil and inserting a knife in the center of the pudding. If the knife does not come out clean, re-cover and bake for additional 5-minute increments until the center shows no liquid custard.
6. Remove from oven and allow to set for 10 minutes.
7. Drizzle warm sauce over bread pudding. Top with whipped cream and serve.

Caramel Sauce

1. While bread pudding is baking, prepare the caramel sauce. Combine ½ cup heavy cream, sugar, corn syrup, and butter in a heavy medium-sized saucepan over medium-high heat. Bring to a boil. Boil for 6–10 minutes, stirring constantly, until it turns a light caramel color. Keep an eye on it; it will foam up near the end, and you may need to reduce the heat.
2. Remove from heat and add the remaining 1 cup cream. It is okay if the caramel clumps up a little as you pour the cream in. Keep stirring and it will smooth out. Keep warm until ready to serve.

COCONUT ALMOND DROPS

Inspired by **Almond Joys**

PREP TIME: 10 MIN · COOK TIME: 15 MIN · CHILL TIME: 40 MIN
TOTAL TIME: 1 HOUR 5 MIN · SERVES 12

This recipe is a family favorite! They are so delicious and easy to make. We prefer these to the actual candy bar.

½ cup light corn syrup

¼ teaspoon salt

10 large marshmallows

2 cups sweetened shredded coconut

½ teaspoon vanilla extract

1 (12-ounce) bag Ghirardelli semisweet chocolate chips

roasted almonds to press in the top (about 12)

1. Either cover a baking sheet with parchment or waxed paper, or use a marble slab. Place your prepared tray in the fridge to chill while you prepare Almond Joys.

2. In a heavy-bottom saucepan over medium heat, combine corn syrup, salt, and marshmallows. Stir until marshmallows are melted, then continue to stir for an additional minute. Remove from stove.

3. Add coconut and vanilla. Stir well and transfer to a bowl. Chill in the fridge for 40 minutes. The mixture needs to get cool enough that it can be rolled into balls.

4. In the meantime, close to when you're ready to make the balls, melt the chocolate chips. You can do this in the microwave or in a double boiler. To use a double boiler, boil water in a pot, then rest a metal bowl over the top. Place the chocolate chips in the metal bowl. Stir until chocolate is melted and smooth. To melt in the microwave, microwave the chocolate in 25–30-second increments, stirring in between, until melted and smooth.

5. Pull out chilled tray and coconut mixture. Roll the coconut mixture into small balls or ovals. Press an almond into the top of each coconut mound. Dip each one in chocolate, then let cool on chilled tray.

NOTES

• The ingredients have to be precise. If you don't use exactly 10 large marshmallows, the consistency is off. Also, make sure you're using shredded coconut, not flakes. The shredded coconut is even better if you chop it more finely in a food processor. And for the chocolate chips, the Ghirardelli brand is worth the extra money.

• To turn these into homemade Mounds, omit the almonds and use dark chocolate chips in place of the semisweet ones.

PEANUT BUTTER CUPS

Inspired by **Reese's**

PREP TIME: 15 MIN · CHILL TIME: 30 MIN
TOTAL TIME: 45 MIN · MAKES 18 FULL-SIZE CUPS OR 36 MINI CUPS

This recipe will satisfy your peanut butter cravings in just minutes, and they taste just like the real thing!

¾ cup crushed graham crackers

1 cup powdered sugar

9 ounces peanut butter (creamy or crunchy)

10 tablespoons butter, divided

12 ounces semisweet chocolate chips (see notes)

1. In a medium-sized bowl, combine graham cracker crumbs and powdered sugar until well blended. Set aside.

2. In a microwave-safe dish, combine peanut butter and 6 tablespoons butter. Cook in the microwave in 15-second increments, stirring in between, until melted and combined. Pour over graham cracker mixture. Continue to stir until well combined. Set aside.

3. In a microwave-safe dish, combine half of the chocolate chips (6 ounces) with 2 tablespoons butter. Cook in the microwave in 15-second increments, stirring in between, until melted and combined. Set aside.

4. Place cupcake liners in a cupcake tin. Using a paintbrush or pastry brush, paint each cupcake liner with melted chocolate. If using full-size cupcake liners, paint about one-third of the way up each cup. If using mini cupcake liners, paint halfway up each cup. Be sure to evenly coat the bottom and sides. You don't need to paint the chocolate super thick, just enough so you don't see any of the liner underneath. Place in the refrigerator to cool for about 5 minutes, or until chocolate hardens.

5. Press about 1 tablespoon graham cracker mixture in each full-size cup (about 1 teaspoon for mini cups), making sure the top is somewhat flat. It doesn't need to be perfect; just make sure you don't go above where you painted the chocolate on the cup. Set aside.

6. Add remaining chocolate chips to remaining melted chocolate in the microwave-safe dish. Melt with remaining 2 tablespoons butter, stirring every 15 seconds.

7. Spoon a little chocolate over each peanut butter cup until the peanut butter filling is completely covered. You can lightly shake or tap the cupcake pan to even out the chocolate over the filling. You want the top of the peanut butter cups to look completely flat.

8. Place in refrigerator or cool area until chocolate hardens, about 20 minutes or until the chocolate is no longer shiny, then serve!

NOTES

• The paintbrush we like to use is a roughly half-inch-wide flat brush.
• The amount of chocolate needed tends to vary each time, so keep a few extra chocolate chips on hand in case you need a bit more.

OATMEAL CRÈME PIES

Inspired by Little Debbie

PREP TIME: 20 MIN · BAKE TIME: 10 MIN · COOL TIME: 15 MIN
TOTAL TIME: 45 MIN · MAKES APPROXIMATELY 18 LARGE SANDWICH COOKIES

These oatmeal cream pies are reminiscent of the cherished Little Debbie version. The soft, chewy oatmeal cookies with a marshmallow cream filling are a timeless favorite.

Oatmeal Cookies

1 cup butter, softened

½ cup granulated sugar

1 cup brown sugar

2 eggs

1 tablespoon molasses

1½ teaspoons vanilla extract

2 cups quick oats

2 cups all-purpose flour

1 teaspoon baking powder

1 teaspoon baking soda

1 teaspoon salt

¾ teaspoon ground cinnamon

Marshmallow Cream Filling

1 cup butter, softened

7 ounces marshmallow fluff

1 teaspoon vanilla extract

1⅓ cups powdered sugar

Oatmeal Cookies

1. Heat oven to 350 degrees F. Line two baking sheets with parchment paper. Set aside.

2. Using a mixer, cream butter, granulated sugar, and brown sugar until light and fluffy. Add eggs one at a time. Mix in molasses and vanilla. Fold in quick oats. Set aside.

3. In a separate bowl, combine flour, baking powder, baking soda, salt, and cinnamon. Slowly add to wet ingredients until combined. Dough will be soft.

4. Use a cookie scoop to place even rounds onto parchment paper. Allow room for cookies to spread. Try to scoop an even number of cookies. Bake for 10 minutes, or until edges are golden brown and centers look set. Let cool completely before removing from pan.

Marshmallow Cream Filling

1. While cookies are cooling, make marshmallow cream filling. Use a mixer to cream butter until soft and fluffy. Fold in marshmallow cream and vanilla. Slowly add powdered sugar and blend until creamy.

2. When cookies are cooled, carefully remove from baking sheets. Spoon a heaping tablespoon of marshmallow filling onto the bottom of one cookie. Place a second cookie on top of cream to make a sandwich.

3. Store extra cookies in an airtight container in the refrigerator.

NOTE

Don't skip the parchment paper. The cookies won't turn out as well if cooked directly on baking sheets.

HOMEMADE MOOSE MUNCH POPCORN

Inspired by **Harry & David**

PREP TIME: 15 MIN · BAKE TIME: 25 MIN · COOL TIME: 1 HOUR
TOTAL TIME: 1 HOUR 40 MIN · SERVES 10–12

This popcorn treat is a perfect blend of sweet caramel, rich milk chocolate, and crunchy nuts. This is an absolute favorite during the holidays and on game nights.

20 cups popped popcorn, kernels removed

½ cup lightly salted whole cashews

½ cup lightly salted whole almonds

½ cup lightly salted peanuts

¾ cup butter

1½ cups brown sugar

½ cup light corn syrup

½ teaspoon baking soda

½ teaspoon salt

1 cup Ghirardelli milk chocolate chips

1. Heat oven to 250 degrees F. Line two large baking sheets with parchment paper. Set aside.

2. Allow popped popcorn to cool for 15 minutes, then combine with nuts in a large bowl. Set aside.

3. In a medium saucepan, combine butter, brown sugar, and corn syrup. Bring to a boil over medium heat, stirring regularly. Boil for 2 minutes. Remove from heat and stir in baking soda and salt. Pour over popcorn and fold until well coated.

4. Pour popcorn onto prepared baking sheets. Bake for 15 minutes. Stir. Bake for another 10 minutes. Remove and let cool.

5. In a microwave-safe bowl, melt chocolate chips in 30-second intervals, stirring in between, until smooth. Use a spoon or fork to drizzle melted chocolate over popcorn.

6. Allow to cool until chocolate hardens, about 10 minutes. Break into bite-size pieces and enjoy!

NOTE

You can use microwaveable bags of unbuttered popcorn if you want. We like Orville Redenbacher's Naturals Simply Salted popcorn. Use 2 bags. Remember to remove the kernels that didn't pop.

SUGAR COOKIES

Inspired by **Swig**

PREP TIME: 20 MIN · COOK TIME: 8 MIN · COOL TIME: 5 MIN · TOTAL TIME: 33 MIN · MAKES 30

Once we tasted these sugar cookies, we were hooked and knew we needed to figure out how to re-create them at home. They're thick, slightly crispy on the outside, chewy on the inside, and, of course, topped with creamy frosting. With all the variations in this recipe, the possibilities are endless! Mix and match cookie and frosting combinations to make your own delicious treats.

Sugar Cookies

1 cup butter, softened

¾ cup vegetable oil

1¼ cups sugar

¾ cup powdered sugar

2 tablespoons water

2 eggs

5½ cups flour

½ teaspoon baking soda

½ teaspoon cream of tartar

1 teaspoon salt

Extra sugar for pressing cookies

Frosting

½ cup butter, softened

¾ cup sour cream

dash of salt

1½–2 pounds powdered sugar

1–2 tablespoons milk, if needed

pink or red food coloring

Sugar Cookies

1. Heat oven to 350 degrees F. Line a baking sheet with a silicone baking mat or use a nonstick baking sheet. Set aside.

2. In a stand mixer or large mixing bowl, combine butter, oil, sugar, powdered sugar, and water. Cream together. Slowly add in eggs.

3. In a medium-sized bowl, combine flour, baking soda, cream of tartar, and salt. Mix well. Slowly add to the butter-sugar mixture until combined and doughy.

4. Roll dough into golf-ball-sized balls and place on prepared baking sheet.

5. Dip the bottom of a glass into excess sugar and press on each dough ball to flatten the cookie. Redip the glass for each cookie. Press lightly because you don't want your cookie to be too thin.

6. Bake for 8–10 minutes or until the bottom is lightly golden brown. Do not overbake.

7. Let cookies remain on the cookie sheet for 5 minutes before moving them to a cooling rack. Cool completely before frosting.

Frosting

1. Cream together butter, sour cream, and salt. Slowly add powdered sugar and mix until desired consistency; you may not need it all. Add milk to thin if needed.

2. Mix in food coloring to the desired hue. Spread over cooled cookies and serve!

NOTES

- Keep the sugar cookies in the freezer after you bake them. When you are ready to eat a cookie, remove it from the freezer and frost it. This is what they do at Swig. The cookie is best when served ice-cold instead of at room temperature. If you've never tried eating cookies this way, pop a few in the freezer and try it. I am a fan!

- Enjoy these cookies with our homemade version of Raspberry Dream soda on page 8.

MALASADAS

Inspired by **Leonard's Bakery**

MALASADAS: PREP TIME: 15 MIN · RISE TIME: 1 HOUR 45 MIN · COOK TIME: 30 MIN
TOTAL TIME: 2 HOURS 30 MIN · MAKES 16
HAUPIA FILLING: PREP TIME: 15 MIN · CHILL TIME: 4 HOURS · TOTAL TIME: 4 HOURS 15 MIN

Malasadas are basically Hawaii's version of a yeast doughnut. Even though malasadas have Portuguese origins (specifically the Azores and Madeira regions) and could be considered more of a Portuguese dessert, they have become widely popular in Hawaii, which is where we were introduced to them. They don't have a hole and, more often than not, are served plain with no filling. Instead of being glazed, they are dusted with sugar. It's like eating a puffy, fried, sugary cloud.

Malasadas

1¼ cups whole milk

1 (.25-ounce) packet active dry yeast (2¼ teaspoons)

¼ cup plus 1 tablespoon sugar, divided

2 eggs

½ cup butter, softened

1 teaspoon salt

4½ cups flour

2 quarts oil, for frying

2 cups granulated sugar, for coating

Malasadas

1. Place the milk in a glass liquid measuring cup. Heat in the microwave for 1 minute. In the bowl of a stand mixer fitted with a dough hook, combine the hot milk with the yeast and 1 tablespoon sugar. Stir lightly. Let sit until the mixture is foamy, about 5 minutes.

2. Beat the remaining ¼ cup sugar, eggs, butter, and salt into the yeast mixture. Add half the flour and mix until combined, then mix in the rest of the flour until the dough pulls away from the sides of the bowl. It's all right if it is still a little tacky. Add more flour, about 2 tablespoons at a time, if the dough is still too sticky.

3. Grease a large bowl with a little oil. Transfer the dough to the bowl and cover with plastic wrap sprayed with cooking spray so the dough won't stick to it if it rises a lot. Let rise at room temperature until it doubles in size, about 1 hour.

4. Turn the dough out onto a well-floured surface and cut into 16 equal pieces. Take each piece and pinch into a ball shape, being careful not to overwork it. Once they're nice and round, pat each piece between your hands, flattening it out a little so it looks like a fat disc.

5. Optional: Place each dough piece on a 4-inch square of parchment paper. This will make it easier to handle them gently and put them in the oil after they rise.

CONTINUED ON NEXT PAGE

DESSERTS

MALASADAS

CONTINUED

6. Cover dough pieces with a kitchen towel and let rise in a warm place until they puff up, about 45 minutes.

7. About 10 minutes before the doughnuts are done rising, heat oil to 350 degrees F. in a deep fryer or Dutch oven. Line a plate or cooling rack with paper towels, for draining. Set aside.

8. Carefully add the malasadas to the oil, a few at a time. Be careful not to crowd them. Cook 45–60 seconds, until the bottoms are deep golden. Use a metal slotted spoon or wooden chopstick to flip, and cook an additional 45–60 seconds, until they're deep golden all over.

9. Use a slotted spoon or oil strainer to carefully remove malasadas to prepared plate or rack. Let cool for a few minutes.

10. Once the malasadas are cool enough to handle (but still very warm), roll in sugar until well coated and set aside. Serve immediately. (If you are going to fill the malasadas, allow them to cool completely before filling and serving.)

Haupia Filling

1 (13.5-ounce) can unsweetened coconut milk

1 cup whole milk

6 large egg yolks

¾ cup sugar

¼ cup cornstarch

¼ teaspoon salt

½ teaspoon vanilla extract

1 teaspoon coconut extract

Haupia Filling

1. Heat coconut milk and whole milk in a heavy saucepan over medium-low heat until hot but not boiling.

2. While milk heats, whisk together yolks, sugar, cornstarch, and salt in a medium-sized mixing bowl until smooth. *Slowly* add hot milk to yolk mixture, whisking constantly.

3. Transfer mixture to saucepan and cook over low heat, stirring constantly, until thickened. Do not boil.

4. Remove from heat and stir in vanilla and coconut extract. Cover and chill 3–4 hours until cold and thick.

5. Place haupia filling in a piping bag. Poke a hole into each malasada with the back of a chopstick or a dowel. Place tip of the bag into the hole and fill until full. Serve immediately.

NOTES

• If your yeast doesn't foam, your yeast is probably bad or nonactive. If that's the case, your dough won't rise and the recipe won't work. It's easier to throw it out and start over than to try and make it work with nonactive yeast.

• To fry your malasadas, consistent heating is key. If you are heating the oil on your stove, use a cooking thermometer to keep the temperature right at 350 degrees F.

• The haupia custard from scratch is *so good* but can also be a little intense and inconsistent. If you want to make things extra easy, you can totally cheat and just use instant coconut pudding or white chocolate pudding with a little coconut extract. Use ½ cup less milk than what the package recommends, or just add milk until you reach the consistency you want. Use 2 or 3 packages to fill all 16 doughnuts.

NOTE

These tasty treats lend themselves well to a wide variety of fillings.

• Chocolate Ganache: Indulge your sweet tooth with a luscious chocolate ganache filling that pairs perfectly with the fluffy doughnut.

• Cinnamon Sugar: Dip your malasadas in cinnamon sugar instead of granulated sugar for a delicious cinnamon variety.

• Coconut Cream: Transport your taste buds to the tropics with a tropical coconut cream filling. Just whip sweetened coconut cream or cream of coconut together with whipping cream until it reaches your desired consistency.

• Cookie Butter: Because you can never go wrong with cookie butter as a filling!

• Custard: Velvety custard is a favorite filling for malasadas, giving them a rich and creamy center.

• Dulce de Leche: The sweet caramel-like flavor complements malasadas beautifully.

• Fruit Preserves: Add a burst of fruity goodness by filling malasadas with your favorite fruit preserves, like raspberry, strawberry, or apricot.

• Lemon Curd: Zesty and tangy lemon curd provides a refreshing contrast to the sweet doughnut.

• Nutella: This hazelnut chocolate spread makes a mouthwatering and addictive filling.

• Whipped Cream and Berries: Top your malasadas with a dollop of whipped cream and fresh berries for a light and fruity twist.

INDEX

RESTAURANT INDEX

ABOUT THE AUTHORS

In 2007, we started Favorite Family Recipes as a way for our own family to share our cherished family recipes with each other. These were the recipes of our grandmothers, our mother, and our aunts. So many of them were carefully kept in an old brown recipe box by our mom. Some were written in pencil or had splashes of food on them. Some were folded and bent. To us, they were buried treasure, and we wanted to preserve them for ourselves, our children, and future grandchildren.

Our fondness for family recipes goes back as long as we can remember. Growing up in our family of seven, the homemade dinners we gathered to share each night were not just about the food. Dinnertime was the one time each day all of us were together. And that was always thanks to our mom—the gatherer—who loved us so much that she made this possible nearly every night throughout our childhoods.

What started as a little online family project grew far more than we could have ever imagined. Favorite Family Recipes has been proudly featured on Disney Parks Blog, Fox News, BuzzFeed, Huffpost, *Parade Magazine*, *Bake It Magazine*, *Grilled Magazine*, *LDSLiving*, BYUtv, Blendtec.com, *The Salt Lake Tribune*, *Good Things Utah*, *KUTV Fresh Living*, Pinners Conference, and KTVB Boise.